Teach Yourself To Play Piano

WILLARD A. PALMER • THOMAS PALMER • MORTON MANUS

What You Need
to Teach Yourself to Play the Piano

1. This INSTRUCTION BOOK. This book is the most carefully planned "teach yourself" method ever devised for the piano. With it you can learn much more than a few simple tunes. If you follow all the instructions carefully, without skipping any pieces or exercises, and if you practice a minimum of one half-hour each day without fail, you will develop enough skill to enjoy playing many pieces for your own amusement as well as for the pleasure of others. You will read music well, and you will understand what you are doing. Once you have attained a certain level of skill, you will not wish to stop with only a half-hour of practice. You will want to play for hours!

2. An INSTRUMENT. You will need an acoustic or electronic piano, or a keyboard that has a piano register. If you use an acoustic spinet, upright, or grand piano, you will have the advantage of unlimited touch sensitivity and the natural feel of the true piano keyboard. Acoustic instruments should be tuned at least twice a year. If you use an electronic instrument, for best results it should have a full-sized, touch-sensitive keyboard. Such instruments are no longer very expensive. Electronic instruments do not require tuning.

3. Optional: The Alfred CD. The recording made especially for use with this book will allow you to hear each piece exactly as it should be played, with or without an instrumental accompaniment. You will enjoy playing along with the piano parts and with the accompaniments. This recording is available from your local music dealer or directly from the publisher.

4. Optional: A STEREO PLAYER. This may be anything from a "boom-box" to an elaborate stereo system. It is best to use a player that uses conventional home current. Adapters are available for most battery operated players. With your stereo system you will be able to hear the music, and/or play along, any of three ways:
   • The RIGHT CHANNEL gives prominence to the piano part YOU will be playing, along with a rhythm (drum) accompaniment.
   • The LEFT CHANNEL gives prominence to an instrumental accompaniment designed to be played along with the piano part.
   • By CENTERING THE CHANNELS, you can hear the piano part and the instrumental accompaniment together, at equal volume.

5. A METRONOME. This is a device that beats time for you to insure that you learn to play in correct rhythm and at the proper tempo (speed). Electronic metronomes are much less expensive and more accurate than mechanical ones. Select one that has a very loud tick, so you can hear it above your own playing.

IMPORTANT! The metronome is for use in preparing the pieces and exercises BEFORE playing them with the CD. Never try to use the metronome with the recording. When you use the CD, the recorded rhythm will always give you the proper tempo.

IMPORTANT! Although this is a "TEACH YOURSELF" book, any student will find it easier with the help of a competent teacher. If you run into difficulties, a teacher is a must. If you find that you are making exceptionally rapid progress on your own, you will certainly learn even more rapidly with professional assistance. Learning music WITH a teacher is always easier than WITHOUT a teacher.

Contents

How to Sit at the Piano

Your POSTURE at the piano is IMPORTANT!

It is much easier to play when your posture is correct.
Please review each of the points listed below each time you play:

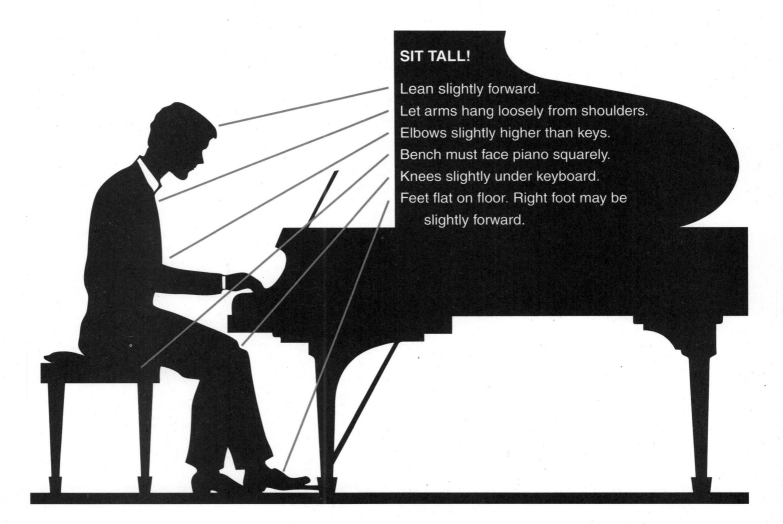

SIT TALL!

Lean slightly forward.
Let arms hang loosely from shoulders.
Elbows slightly higher than keys.
Bench must face piano squarely.
Knees slightly under keyboard.
Feet flat on floor. Right foot may be
    slightly forward.

Tuning Your Instrument Track 1*

YOUR INSTRUMENT MUST BE IN TUNE WITH THE RECORDING!

At the beginning of the recording you will hear a pitch sounded for about 20 seconds. This is the standard A-440 pitch that piano tuners usually use.

If you are using an acoustic piano, you will want to check to see that your instrument is in tune with the recording. Playing a piano that is IN TUNE is important in training your ear as you learn, so please do not neglect this important step! If your instrument is not in tune with the recording, have a piano tuner tune your instrument to the pitch sounded on the recording, not just to A-440 pitch. Alternatively, if your CD player has a tuning adjustment, you can adjust the pitch of the A sounded on the recording to the pitch of the A above middle C on your piano.

Most touch-sensitive electronic instruments have a tuning device that will quickly and easily adjust the pitch of the instrument to match the recording. See your owner's manual.

 * This symbol indicates that the selection is included on the CD recording.
    The number is the "track" number, indicating the order of pieces.

How the Fingers Are Numbered

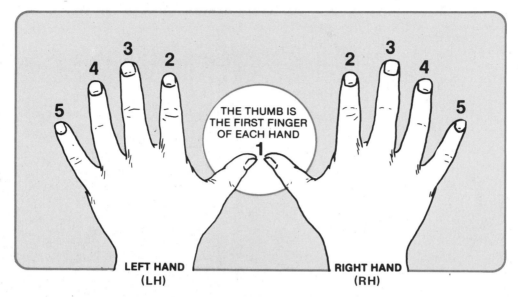

THE THUMB IS THE FIRST FINGER OF EACH HAND

LEFT HAND (LH)   **RIGHT HAND (RH)**

As you study the above diagram, practice moving each finger as you say its number aloud, then proceed to the following exercise:

To prepare for this exercise, press the hands flatly together with all fingers touching, in a "prayer position."

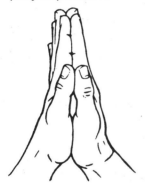

Now slowly bring the palms apart, with fingertips touching, until all fingers are in a curved position.

1. With all the other fingers still touching, tap the thumbs together four times, saying "ONE-ONE-ONE-ONE." Move the thumbs 3 or more inches apart between each tap.

2. Tap the 2nd fingers together four times, saying "TWO-TWO-TWO-TWO."

3. Tap the 3rd fingers together. Say "THREE-THREE-THREE-THREE."

4. Tap the 4th fingers together. Say "FOUR-FOUR-FOUR-FOUR."
   You will notice that the 4th finger is more difficult to move than the other fingers. You may be able to move the 4th fingers only a short distance apart (see page 84).

5. Tap the 5th fingers together. Say "FIVE-FIVE-FIVE-FIVE."

Shake the hands out vigorously, dangling loosely from the wrists, as shown below.
Count "ONE-TWO-THREE-FOUR."

DANGLE FROM WRISTS

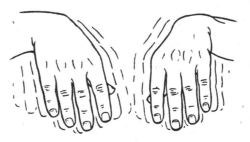

SHAKE OUT HANDS

Repeat this page several times.

How Piano Tones Are Made

When you play a key, a hammer inside your piano touches a string to make a tone.
When you drop into a key with a LITTLE weight, you make a SOFT tone.
When you use MORE weight, you make a LOUDER tone.

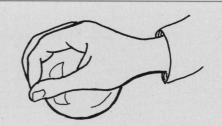

Curve your fingers when you play!
Pretend you have a bubble in your hand.
Hold the bubble gently so it doesn't break!

Dynamic Signs

Dynamic signs tell how loud or soft to play. They are abbreviations of Italian words.

f = FORTE, pronounced "FOR-tay." It means LOUD.
   Drop into the key with considerable weight.

mf = MEZZO FORTE, pronounced "MET-so FOR-tay." It means MODERATELY LOUD.
   Drop into the key with less weight.

p = PIANO. It means SOFT.
   Drop into the key with only a *little weight*.

Dynamic Exercise

Choose any white key near the middle of the keyboard. Using RH 3 (Right Hand 3rd finger),

1. Play the key *f* (LOUD). Use considerable weight to play it 4 times FORTE.
2. Play it again, *mf* (MODERATELY LOUD). Use less weight to play it 4 times MEZZO FORTE.
3. Play it again, *p* (SOFT). Use only a little weight to play it 4 times PIANO.

Repeat the entire exercise, using LH 3 (Left Hand 3rd finger).
Choose any white key near the middle of the keyboard and play it 4 times *f,* 4 times *mf* and 4 times *p.*

Four Good Reasons for Playing with Curved Fingers

1. When the fingers are straight, each finger has a different length.

When the fingers are curved, each finger has, in effect, the same length.

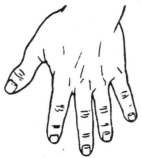

2. If your fingers are straight, the thumb cannot be properly used.

Curved fingers bring the thumb into the correct playing position.

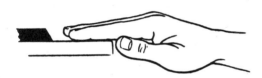

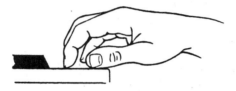

3. Straight fingers will bend at the first joint, opposite to the motion of the key, delaying key response.

With curved fingers, keys respond instantly. You are IN CONTROL when you CURVE!

4. Moving over the keys will require passing the thumb *under* the fingers and crossing fingers *over* the thumb. Curved fingers provide an "ARCH" that makes this motion possible.

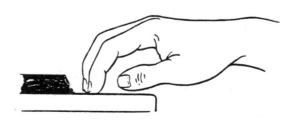

VERY IMPORTANT! Keep fingernails reasonably SHORT. It is impossible to curve fingers properly with long fingernails.

BE KIND TO YOUR HANDS!

No part of the body takes more abuse than the hands. We wear shoes on our feet to protect them against the rough surfaces they walk on. Our hands are almost constantly exposed to the elements and to the rough things we do to them. Gloves are usually worn only to keep the hands warm in cold weather.

If you want to keep your hands in playing condition, it is best to wear gloves when you are lifting large, heavy objects, as well as when you are working with rough tools, screwdrivers, pliers, wrenches, pruning shears, spades, and even vacuum cleaners.

Preliminary Exercises

No. 1

a) Holding your arms in playing position, palms downward, clench both hands tightly, making two fists. Hold while you count "ONE-TWO."

MAKE TIGHT
FISTS

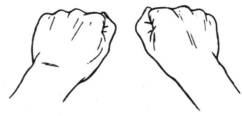

PALMS
DOWN

b) SNAP fingers quickly outward, opening both hands. Do this with great vigor. Hold this position with all fingers extended. Count "THREE-FOUR." Do this several times.

SNAP
FINGERS OPEN

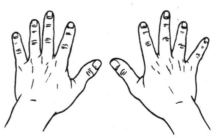

PALMS
DOWN

c) Shake out both hands, dangling from the wrists. Count "ONE-TWO-THREE-FOUR."

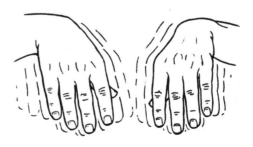

USE A LITTLE WARM WATER

Before practicing, it is good to soak the hands for a few minutes in warm water. This promotes circulation. Many concert pianists use very warm water on their hands before beginning to play. Towel the hands vigorously until they are dry, then hold your arms out with the hands dangling from the wrist, and shake out your hands rapidly for a few moments.

No. 2

a) Repeat the beginning of the previous exercise, with PALMS UPWARD. Clench both hands, making two fists. Hold and count "ONE-TWO."

MAKE TIGHT
FISTS

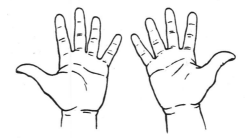

PALMS
UP

b) SNAP the fingers outward (palms up), opening both hands. Hold fingers outward as you count "THREE-FOUR." Do this several times.

SNAP
FINGERS OPEN

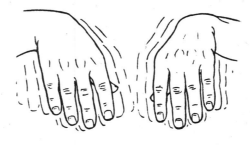

PALMS
UP

c) Turn hands over, palms down, hands dangling from the wrists, and shake out. Count "ONE-TWO-THREE-FOUR."

A Beneficial Hand Massage

1. Place the back of the left hand in the palm of the right hand, relaxed and flat.
2. With the thumb of the right hand, massage the left hand along the ridge of the fingers and along the fleshy part of the base of the thumb. Do not use excessive pressure, or you may bruise the hand. Continue this for about 30 seconds.

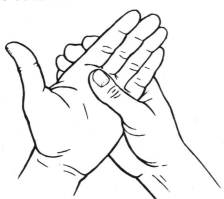
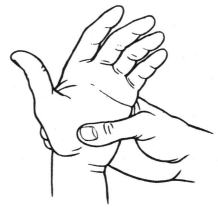

3. Reverse hands, massaging the right hand with the left.
4. Shake out the hands vigorously for several seconds.

This exercise should be beneficial to circulation and should make the hands more flexible.

The Keyboard

The keyboard is made up of white keys and black keys.
The black keys are in groups of 2's and 3's.

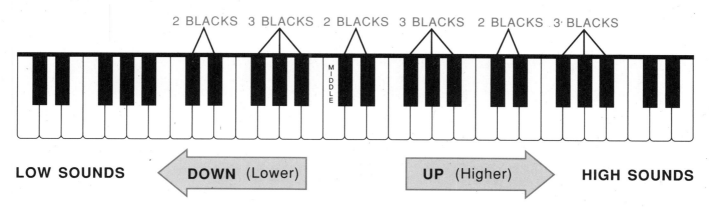

2 BLACKS 3 BLACKS 2 BLACKS 3 BLACKS 2 BLACKS 3 BLACKS

LOW SOUNDS ← DOWN (Lower)   UP (Higher) → HIGH SOUNDS

On the keyboard, DOWN is to the LEFT, and UP is the RIGHT.
As you move LEFT, the tones sound LOWER. As you move RIGHT, the tones sound HIGHER.

In just a few minutes, you can learn the name of every key on your piano!

Piano keys are named for the first seven letters of the alphabet, beginning with **A.**

A B C D E F G

Each white key is recognized by its position in or next to a black key group!
For example: **A**'s are found between the **TOP TWO KEYS** of each **3 BLACK KEY GROUP.**

Play the following. Use LH 3 for keys below the middle of the keyboard.
Use RH 3 for keys above the middle of the keyboard.

Say the name of each key aloud as you play! Play all keys *mf* (moderately loud).

Play all the **A**'s on your piano.

Play all the **B**'s.
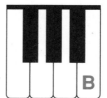

Play all the **C**'s.
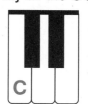

Play all the **D**'s.
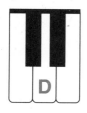

Play all the **E**'s.

Play all the **F**'s.

Play all the **G**'s.

Now you can name every white key!

REMEMBER! The key names are **A B C D E F G,** used over and over!

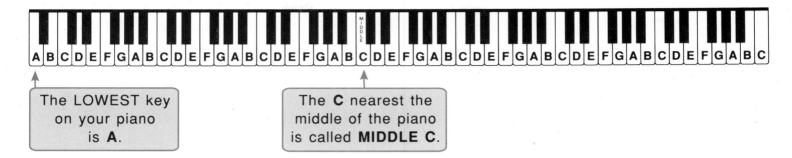

The LOWEST key
on your piano
is **A.**

The **C** nearest the
middle of the piano
is called **MIDDLE C.**

Beginning to Play ~~Track 2~~ (DEMO ONLY)*

Place the RH on the keyboard so the **1st FINGER** falls on **MIDDLE C.**
Let the remaining 4 fingers fall naturally on the next 4 white keys.

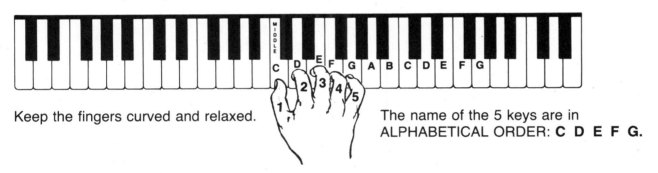

Keep the fingers curved and relaxed.

The name of the 5 keys are in
ALPHABETICAL ORDER: **C D E F G.**

1. Play **C, E, G,** one key at a time, with RH 1, 3, 5. Play *mf* (moderately loud).
2. Move the hand to a position one white key to the right and play **D, F, A** with 1, 3, 5.
3. Continue up the keyboard, playing **E, G, B,** then **F, A, C,** then **G, B, D,** then **A, C, E,** then **B, D, F.**
   Stop after you play the next higher **C, E, G.**

Place the LH on the keyboard so the **5th FINGER** falls on the **C BELOW** (to the left of) **MIDDLE C.**
Let the remaining fingers fall naturally on the next 4 white keys.

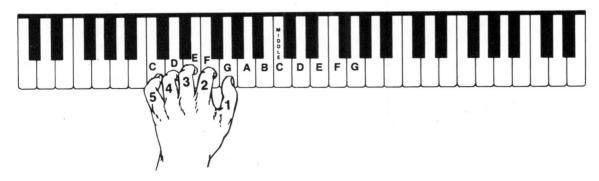

4. Play **C, E, G,** one key at a time, with LH 5, 3, 1. Play *mf*.
5. Move the hand one white key to the right. Play **D, F, A,** with 5, 3, 1.
6. Continue up the keyboard, playing **E, G, B,** then **F, A, C,** then **G, B, D,** then **A, C, E,** then **B, D, F.**
   Stop after you play the next higher **C, E, G.**
7. Repeat steps 1 through 6, playing *f* (loud). Repeat again, playing *p* (soft).

*Do not play along with the recording when the exercise is marked "DEMO ONLY."

Right Hand C Position

Place the RH on the keyboard so the **1st FINGER** falls on **MIDDLE C.**
Let the remaining 4 fingers fall naturally on the next 4 white keys.
Keep the fingers curved and relaxed.

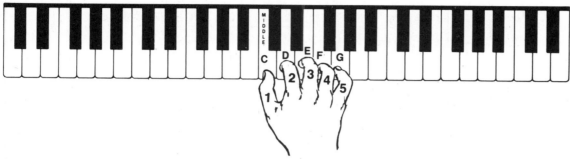

Notes for this position are written on the TREBLE STAFF.

The TREBLE STAFF has 5 lines and 4 spaces.
Middle **C** is written on a short line below the staff, called a *leger* line. **D** is written in the space below the staff.
Each next higher note is written on the next higher line or space.

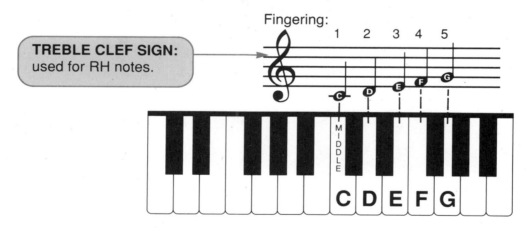

Fingering:

TREBLE CLEF SIGN:
used for RH notes.

RIGHT HAND WARM-UP 🎵 Track 3 (DEMO ONLY—do not play along with recording.)

Play the following *WARM-UP*. Say the name of each note aloud as you play.
Repeat until you can play smoothly and evenly. As the notes go higher on the keyboard, they are written higher on the staff!

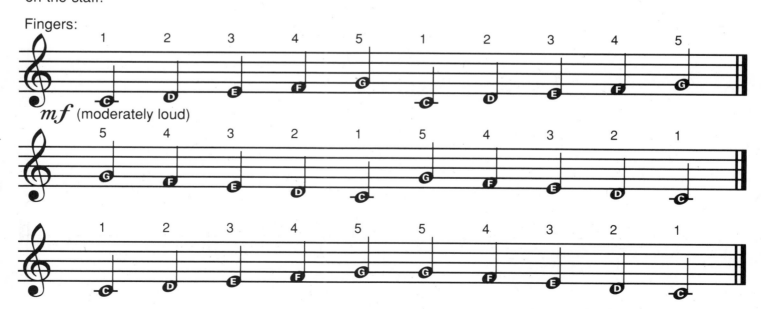

Quarter Notes & Half Notes

Music is made up of **short** tones and **long** tones. We write these tones in **notes**, and we measure their lengths by **counting**. The combining of notes into patterns is called **RHYTHM**.

Quarter Note
a **short** note.

COUNT: "1"

Half Note
a **long** note.

COUNT: "1 - 2"

Now you are ready to use your metronome.

The metronome will help you play rhythm evenly, and at the proper **tempo** (speed). Before each exercise or piece, you will be given a metronome setting.

For example, ♩ = 80 tells you to set the metronome at 80 and play one QUARTER NOTE for EACH TICK. This will be 80 ticks per minute.

Clap the following rhythm. Clap **ONCE** for each note, counting aloud.
Note how the **BAR LINES** divide the music into **MEASURES** of equal duration.

♩ = 80   Clap one quarter note for each tick of the metronome.
Let the metronome tick TWICE for the final HALF NOTE.

←——— MEASURE ———→ BAR LINE ←— MEASURE ——→ BAR LINE ←— MEASURE ——→ BAR LINE ←— MEASURE ——→ DOUBLE BAR used at the end

ODE TO JOY *(Theme from Beethoven's 9th Symphony)* Track 4

Play very slowly at first, about ♩ = 50 or slower.
Gradually increase speed to ♩ = 92, **then PLAY ALONG WITH THE RECORDING!**
Listen for 2 measures (8 beats) of rhythm introduction, then play.

To play along with the rhythm and piano part, tune your stereo to the RIGHT channel.
To play along with the accompaniment only, tune to the LEFT channel.
To play along with all parts, CENTER the stereo channels.

Fingers:

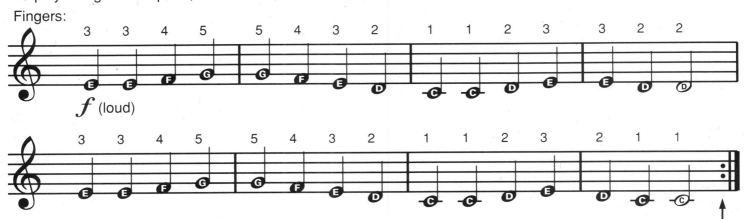

The DOUBLE DOTS mean
REPEAT FROM THE BEGINNING.

Left Hand C Position

Place the LH on the keyboard so the **5th FINGER** falls on the **C BELOW** (to the left of) **MIDDLE C**.
Let the remaining fingers fall naturally on the next 4 white keys.
Keep the fingers curved and relaxed.

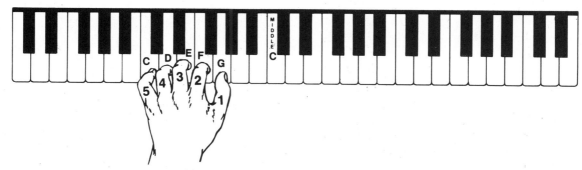

NOTES for this position are written on the BASS STAFF.

The BASS STAFF also has 5 lines and 4 spaces.
The **C**, played by 5, is written on the 2nd space of the staff.
Each next higher note is written on the next higher line or space.

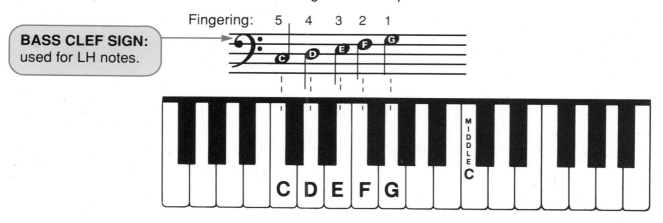

BASS CLEF SIGN:
used for LH notes.

LEFT HAND WARM-UP Track 5 (DEMO ONLY)

Begin very slowly. Set the metronome at ♩ = 50, or slower, if necessary.
Gradually increase tempo to ♩ = 80.

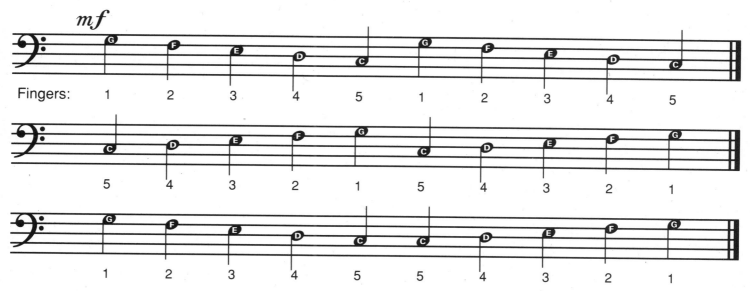

When notes are BELOW the MIDDLE LINE of the staff, the stems usually point UP.
When notes are ON or ABOVE the MIDDLE LINE, the stems usually point DOWN.

The Whole Note

> ## Whole Note
> a **very long** note. 𝅝
>
> **COUNT:** "1 - 2 - 3 - 4"

Clap the following rhythm. Clap **ONCE** for each note, counting aloud.

♩ = 50. Hold the whole note for 4 ticks of the metronome.

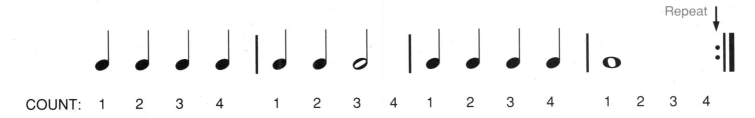

COUNT: 1   2   3   4   1   2   3   4   1   2   3   4   1   2   3   4

AURA LEE   🄯 Track 6

This melody was made into a popular song, *"LOVE ME TENDER,"* sung by Elvis Presley.

Play slowly, at first, about ♩ = 50, or slower.

Gradually increase tempo to ♩ = 92, **then play along with the recording.**

Listen for 2 measures (8 beats) of rhythm introduction, then play.

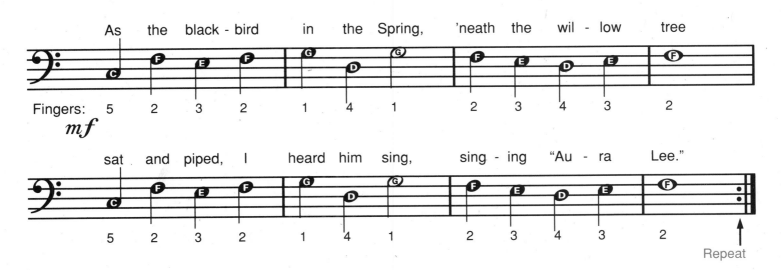

OPTIONAL: 2nd time play with LH one octave (8 notes higher).

The Grand Staff

The BASS STAFF & TREBLE STAFF, when joined together with a BRACE, make up the **GRAND STAFF**.

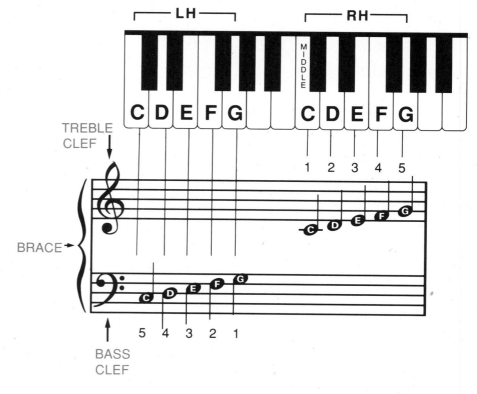

TREBLE CLEF

BRACE →

BASS CLEF

TIME SIGNATURE

Music has numbers at the beginning called the **TIME SIGNATURE**.

$\frac{4}{4}$ means **4** beats to each measure

means a **QUARTER NOTE** ♩ gets one beat.

PLAYING ON THE GRAND STAFF Track 7

Only the starting finger number for each hand is given.

Play slowly, at first, about ♩ = 50, or slower.
Gradually increase tempo to ♩ = 92. Play with recording.

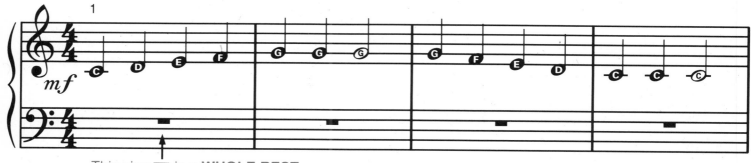

This sign ▬ is a **WHOLE REST**.
LH is silent a whole measure!

RH silent a whole measure.

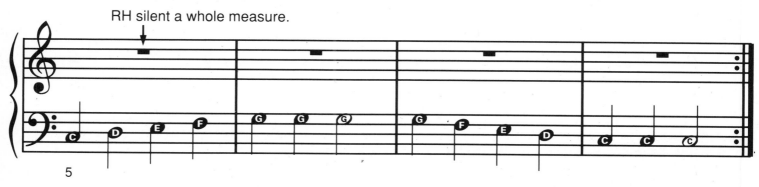

Finger "Aerobics" 🎵 Track 8

FINGER AEROBICS, practiced daily, will improve your playing skills, and will make playing the pieces in this book much easier.

You may play the hands separately at first, if you wish, as slowly as you like.

Because the notes are in "contrary motion," that is, the RH goes up when the LH goes down, and vice versa, it will not be difficult to play the hands together. The hands play identical fingering at all times: thumbs play together, 2nd fingers play together, etc.

The signs *p* - *mf* - *f* indicate that the exercise is repeated 3 times, and you should play *piano* (soft) the first time, *mezzo forte* (moderately loud) the 2nd time, and *forte* (loud) the 3rd time.

After you have the hands together, begin playing at ♩ = 80. Gradually increase the tempo to ♩ = 120. From here on the final tempo is always the tempo used to play with the **recording**.

No. 1

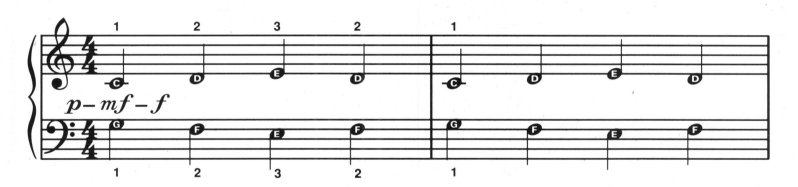

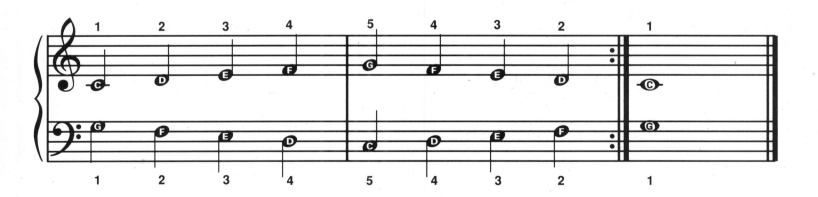

There are MORE FINGER AEROBICS in the back of this book, beginning on page 85.
If you will practice No. 2 and No. 3 each day, you will strengthen your weakest fingers (4 & 5).
For an explanation of why this is needed, please read page 84.

Melodic Intervals: 2nds

Distances from one note to another are measured in **INTERVALS**, called 2nds, 3rds, etc.
Notes played SEPARATELY make a **MELODY**.
We call the intervals between these notes **MELODIC INTERVALS**.

 The distance from any white key to the next white key, up or down, is called a **2nd**.

> 2nds are written LINE-SPACE or SPACE-LINE.

Play, saying "UP a 2nd," etc.

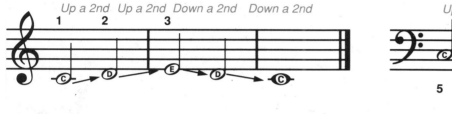

SECONDS  Track 9

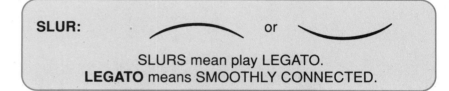

SLUR: _____ or _____

SLURS mean play LEGATO.
LEGATO means SMOOTHLY CONNECTED.

Drop into the first key of each slurred pair of notes. Let the wrist rise to lead the hand
as you lift gracefully off of the 2nd note of each pair.

f - p means play _forte_ the 1st time, _piano_ the 2nd time.

Play slowly at first, about ♩ = 50. Gradually increase tempo to ♩ = 80.

REMEMBER! You can hear the piano part alone on the right stereo channel. You can hear the accompaniment
alone on the left stereo channel. If you center the stereo channels, you will hear both the piano and the accompaniment.

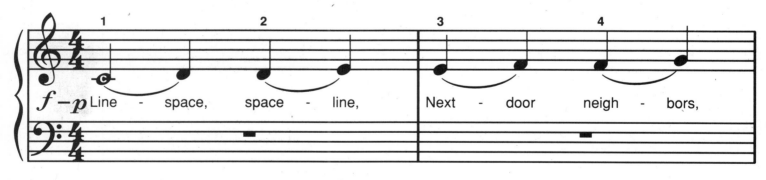

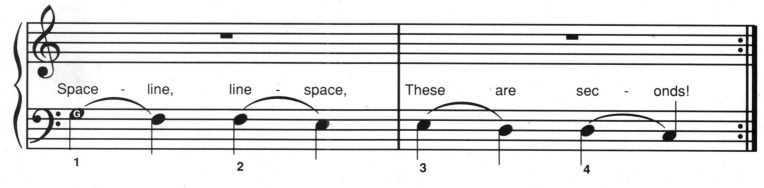

IMPORTANT! To improve your skill at playing 2nds, practice FINGER AEROBIC No. 4 on page 86.

THE SECOND STREET BAND Track 10

This piece uses only repeated notes and 2nds. Begin as slowly as you wish.
Gradually increase tempo to ♩ = 120.

The right channel has piano and drums. When you add the left channel, you will hear a jazzy flute accompaniment. To hear the piano and the accompaniment, center the channels.

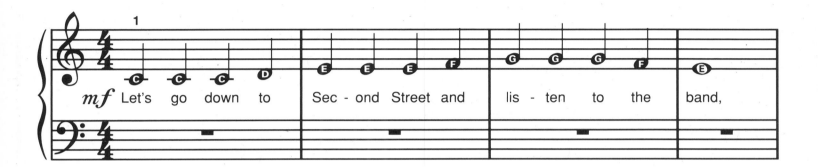

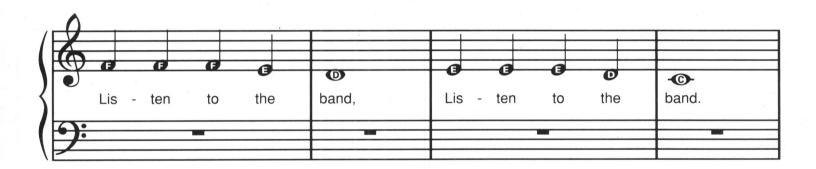

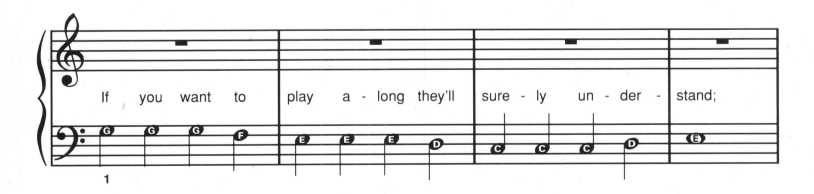

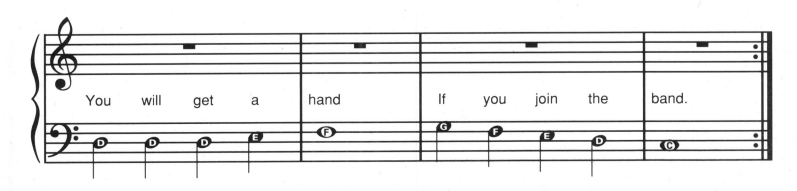

Melodic Intervals: 3rds

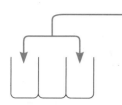

When you skip a white key, the interval is a **3rd**.

3rds are written LINE-LINE or SPACE-SPACE.

Play, saying "UP a 3rd," etc.

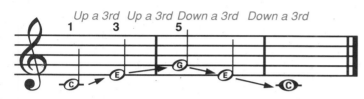

THIRDS  Track 11

Set the metronome at ♩ = 60, or slower, and play several times.
Practice at gradually increased speeds.

Recording tempo ♩ = 104

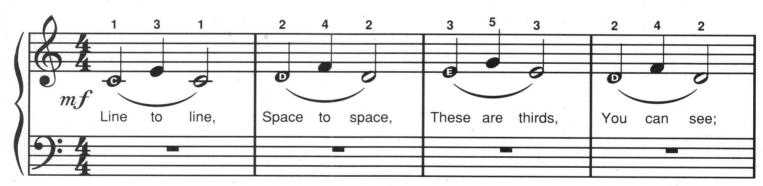

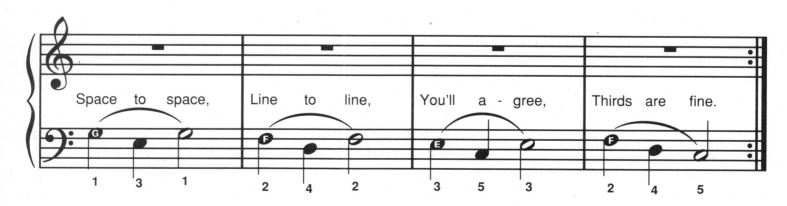

IMPORTANT! To improve your skill at playing 3rds, practice FINGER AEROBIC No. 5 on page 86.

ROCK-ALONG

Track 12

This piece uses only repeated notes and 3rds. Begin as slowly as you wish.

Recording tempo ♩ = 120

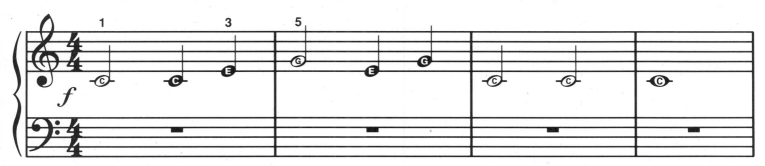

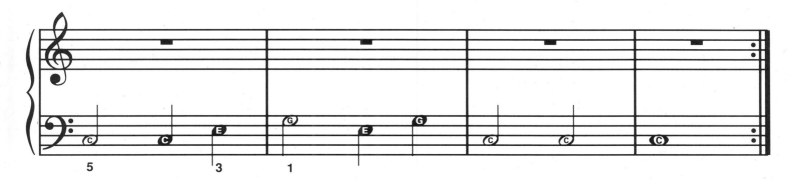

MEXICAN HAT DANCE

Track 13

This piece combines 3rds and 2nds. Lift your hand from the wrist for one count on each quarter rest.

Recording tempo ♩ = 120

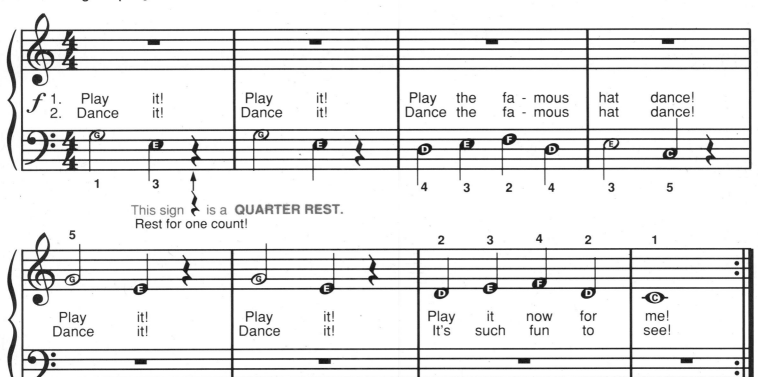

This sign is a **QUARTER REST.**
Rest for one count!

Melodic Intervals: 4ths

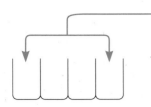

When you skip 2 white key, the interval is a **4th**.

> 4ths are written LINE-SPACE or SPACE-LINE.

Play, saying "UP a 4th," etc.

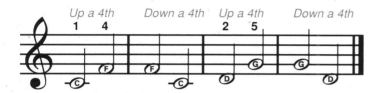

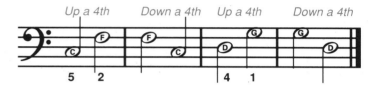

PLAY A FOURTH *Track 14*

Begin at ♩ = 60, or slower.
Increase speed to ♩ = 104.

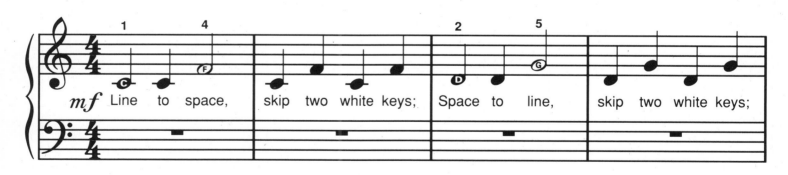

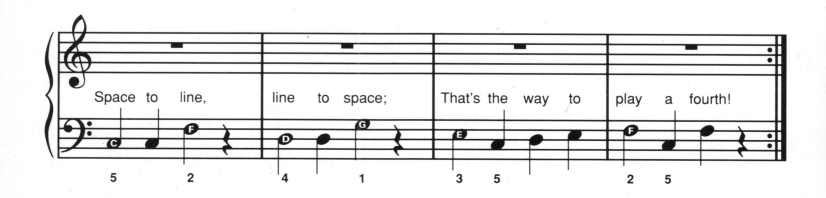

RHYTHM MAN Track 15

Find the 4ths before you play!

Begin at ♩ = 60 or slower.

Gradually increase speed to ♩ = 120.

8va Placed OVER the staff means PLAY THE NOTES ONE OCTAVE (8 notes) HIGHER THAN WRITTEN.

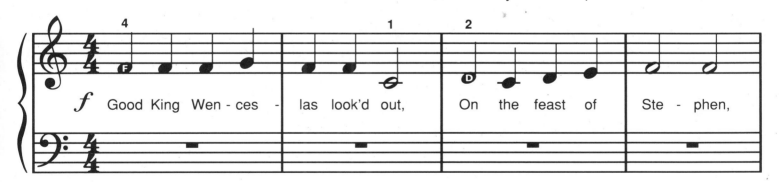

GOOD KING WENCESLAS Track 16

Find the 4ths before you play!

Practice first at ♩ = 60, or slower.

Gradually increase speed to ♩ = 104.

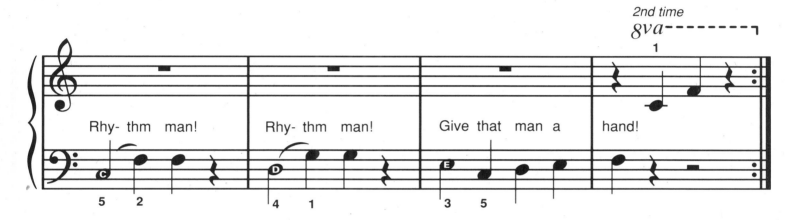

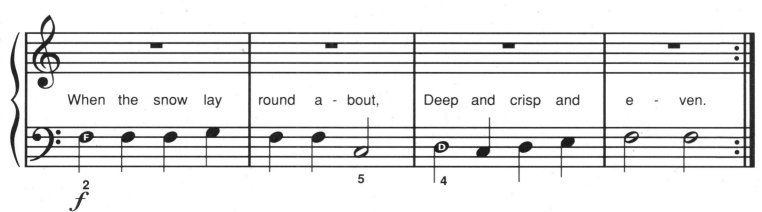

Melodic Intervals: 5ths

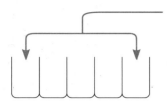

When you skip 3 white keys, the interval is a **5th**.

5ths are written LINE-LINE or SPACE-SPACE.

Play, saying "UP a 5th," etc.

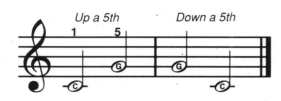

FIFTHS   Track 17

Begin at ♩ = 80 or slower.

When you play with the recording, begin by playing several times with the RIGHT CHANNEL ONLY!

2nd time play 1 octave (8 notes) lower.

Recording tempo ♩ = 120

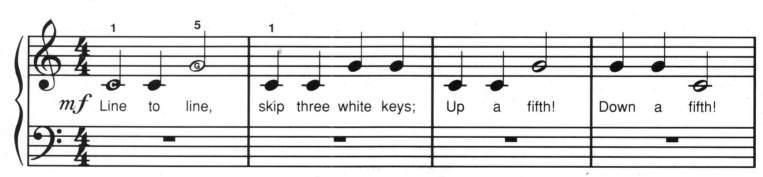

mf Line to line,   skip three white keys;   Up a fifth!   Down a fifth!

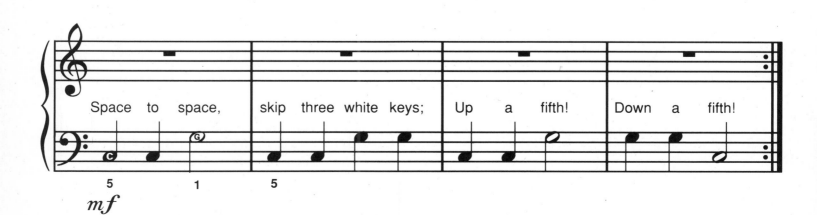

Space to space,   skip three white keys;   Up a fifth!   Down a fifth!

mf

MY FIFTH Track 18

Find the 5ths before you play!
Begin as slowly as you wish.

Recording tempo ♩ = 120

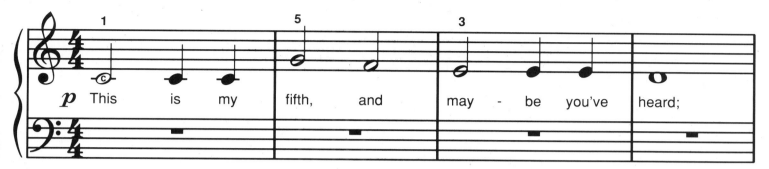

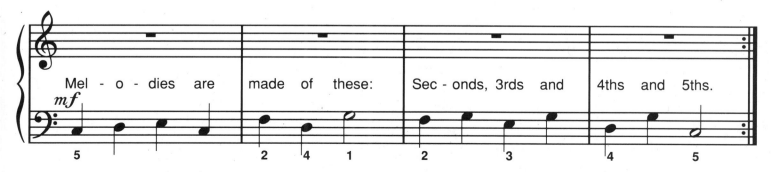

Melodic Interval Review Track 19

So far, you have played MELODIC INTERVALS (notes played SEPARATELY, to make a MELODY).

Name all the MELODIC INTERVALS in this piece before you play it.

Begin at ♩ = 80
Recording tempo ♩ = 120

IMPORTANT! To improve your skill at playing melodic intervals, practice FINGER AEROBIC No. 6 on page 87.

Harmonic Intervals: 2nds & 3rds

Notes played **TOGETHER** make **HARMONY**.
We call the intervals between these notes **HARMONIC INTERVALS**.
Play these HARMONIC **2nds** & **3rds**. Listen to the sound of each interval.

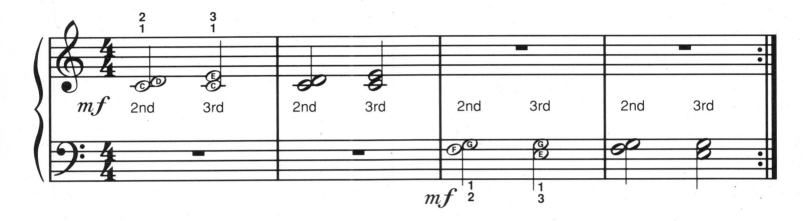

Quiet River Track 20

Play this piece SLOWLY. The recording accompaniment will give you a 2 measure introduction (instead of a count off), at ♩ = 80.

You have made great progress! From here on, you will be playing pieces with hands together!

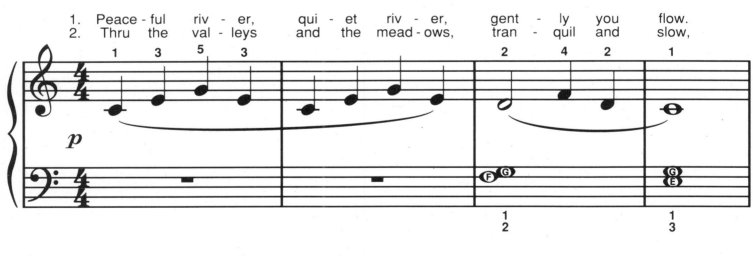

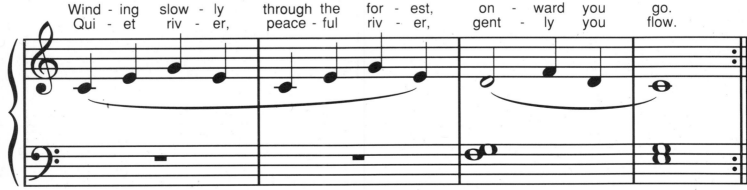

Harmonic 4ths & 5ths

Play these HARMONIC **4ths** & **5ths**. Listen to the sound of each interval.

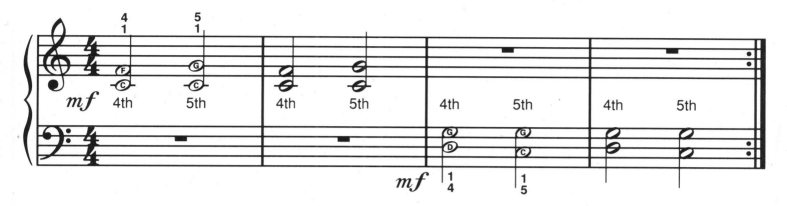

TIED NOTES: When notes on the *same* line or space are joined with a curved line, we call them **TIED NOTES**.

The key is held down for the COMBINED VALUES OF BOTH NOTES!

COUNT: "1 - 2 - 3 - 4, 1 - 2 - 3 - 4."

LITTLE THINGS 🎵 Track 21

Words by Julia Carney

Play hands separately at first, then together.

Notice that the LH harmonic intervals are in numerical order: after you play the G alone, you will play a 2nd, 3rd, 4th, and 5th.

The recording will play a 4 measure introduction at ♩ = 104.

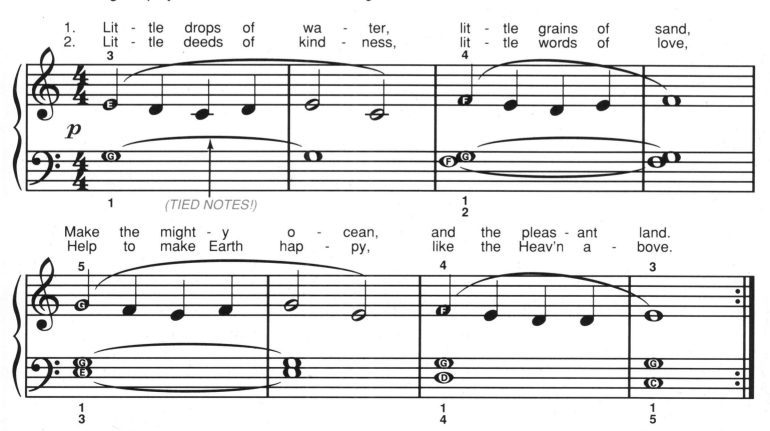

1. Lit - tle drops of wa - ter, lit - tle grains of sand,
2. Lit - tle deeds of kind - ness, lit - tle words of love,

(TIED NOTES!)

Make the might - y o - cean, and the pleas - ant land.
Help to make Earth hap - py, like the Heav'n a - bove.

IMPORTANT! To improve your skill at playing harmonic intervals, practice FINGER AEROBIC No. 7 on page 87.

JINGLE BELLS

Track 22

From here on, you will usually be given only the metronome tempo of the recording.
You may begin each piece or exercise as slowly as you wish, but ALWAYS use the metronome at first, to ensure playing in perfect rhythm.

The recording will play a 4-measure introduction at ♩ = 132

The Sharp Sign

 The SHARP SIGN
before a note means
play the next key to the right,
whether BLACK OR WHITE.

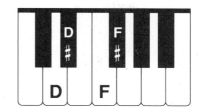

When a SHARP SIGN appears before a note,
it applies to that note for the rest of the measure.

MONEY CAN'T BUY EV'RYTHING!

Begin at ♩ = 80 or slower.
Recording tempo ♩ = 138

The C Major Chord

A chord is three or more notes played together.
The **C MAJOR CHORD** is made of three notes: **C E G.**

Be sure to play all three chord notes exactly together,
with fingers nicely curved.

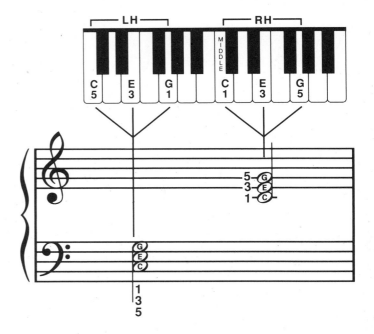

C MAJOR CHORDS for LH

Play & count.

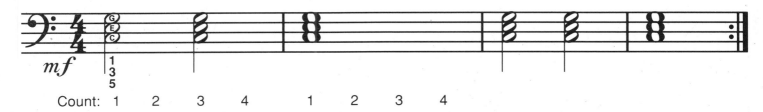

C MAJOR CHORDS for RH

Play & count.

C MAJOR CHORDS for BOTH HANDS

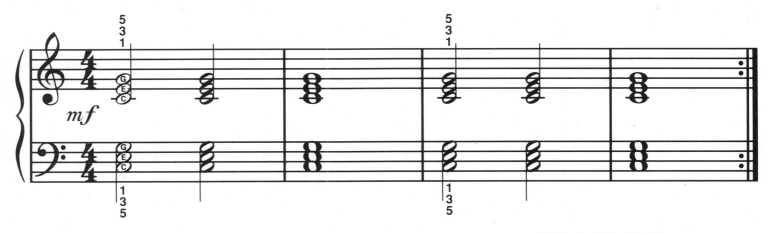

IMPORTANT! To improve your skill at playing the C major chord, practice FINGER AEROBICS
Nos. 8 & 9 on page 88.

BROTHER JOHN Track 24

READ BY PATTERNS! For RH, think: "C, up a 2nd, up a 2nd, down a 3rd," etc. THINK the pattern, then PLAY it!

Recording tempo ♩ = 104

You will hear a 2 measure intro, with rhythm & bells.

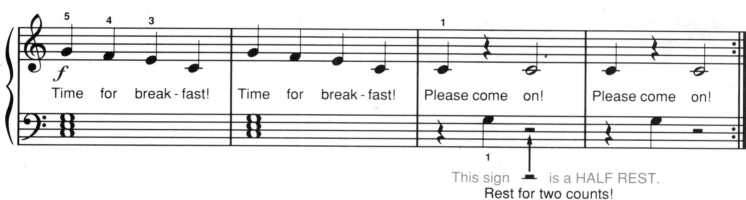

This sign ▬ is a HALF REST.
Rest for two counts!

HERE'S A HAPPY SONG! Track 25

READ BY PATTERNS! For LH, think: "G, down a 2nd, down a 2nd, up a 2nd," etc.

Begin at ♩ = 60 or slower.

Recording tempo ♩ = 120

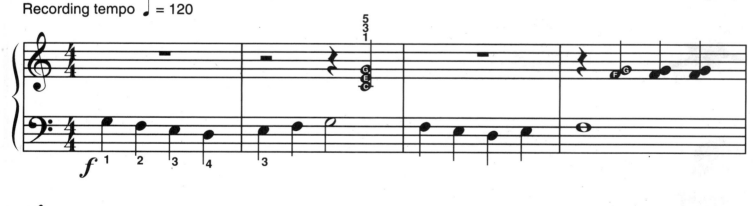

Introducing 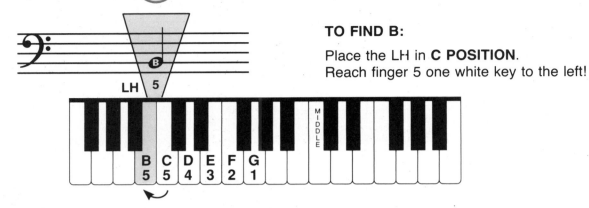 B for Left Hand

TO FIND B:

Place the LH in **C POSITION**.
Reach finger 5 one white key to the left!

Play slowly. Say the note names as you play.

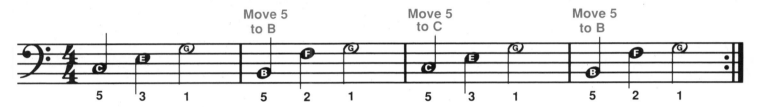

Two Important Chords

Two frequently used chords are **C MAJOR** & **G⁷**.

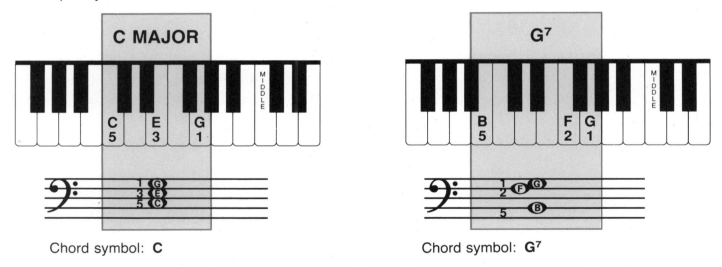

Chord symbol: **C**

Chord symbol: **G⁷**

Chord symbols are always used in popular music to identify chord names.

Practice changing from the C chord to the G⁷ chord and back again:

1. The 1st finger plays G in both chords.
2. The 2nd finger plays F in the G⁷ chord.
3. Only the 5th finger moves out of C POSITION (down to B) for G⁷.

IMPORTANT! To improve your skill at playing the G7 chord, practice FINGER AEROBICS Nos. 10 & 11 on page 89.

MERRILY WE ROLL ALONG

Track 26

Play the RH & LH separately at first, then together. Practice the RH *mf* and the LH *p*.
The melody should always be clearly heard above the accompaniment.

Practice at ♩ = 60 or slower.
Recording tempo ♩ = 120

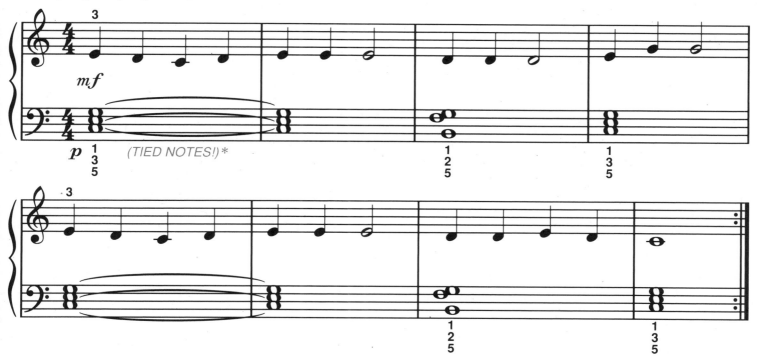

(TIED NOTES!)*

LARGO (*from "THE NEW WORLD"*)

Track 27

This melody is also known as GOING HOME.
The word LARGO means "very slow."

Recording tempo ♩ = 60

Dvořák

1 plays G♯ **

*Review page 27.
**C E G♯ is a C AUGMENTED (enlarged) CHORD.

Introducing (B) for Right Hand

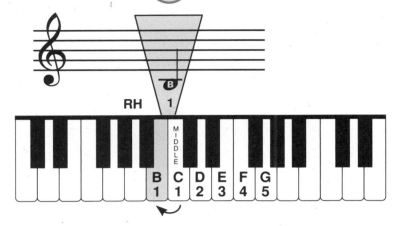

RH

TO FIND B:

Place the RH in **C POSITION**.
Reach finger 1 one white key to the left!

Play slowly. Say the note names as you play.

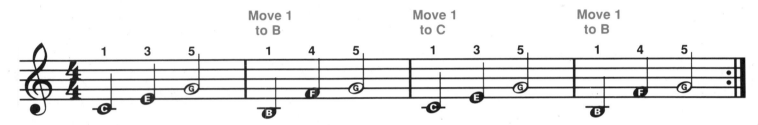

C & G⁷ Chords for Right Hand

It is important to be able to play all chords with the RIGHT hand as well as the LEFT.
Chords are used in either or both hands in popular and classical music.

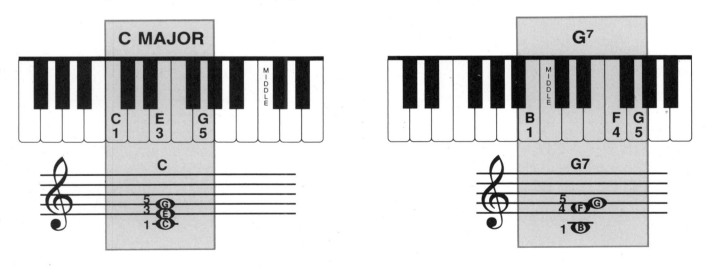

Practice changing from the C chord to the G⁷ chord and back again!

1. The 5th finger plays G in both chords.
2. The 4th finger plays F in the G⁷ chord.
3. Only the 1st finger moves out of C POSITION (down to B) for G⁷.

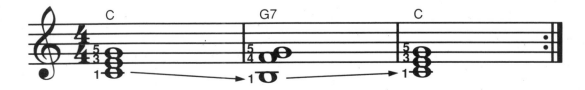

MARY ANN

Track 28

Practice at ♩ = 80 or slower.

Recording tempo ♩ = 120

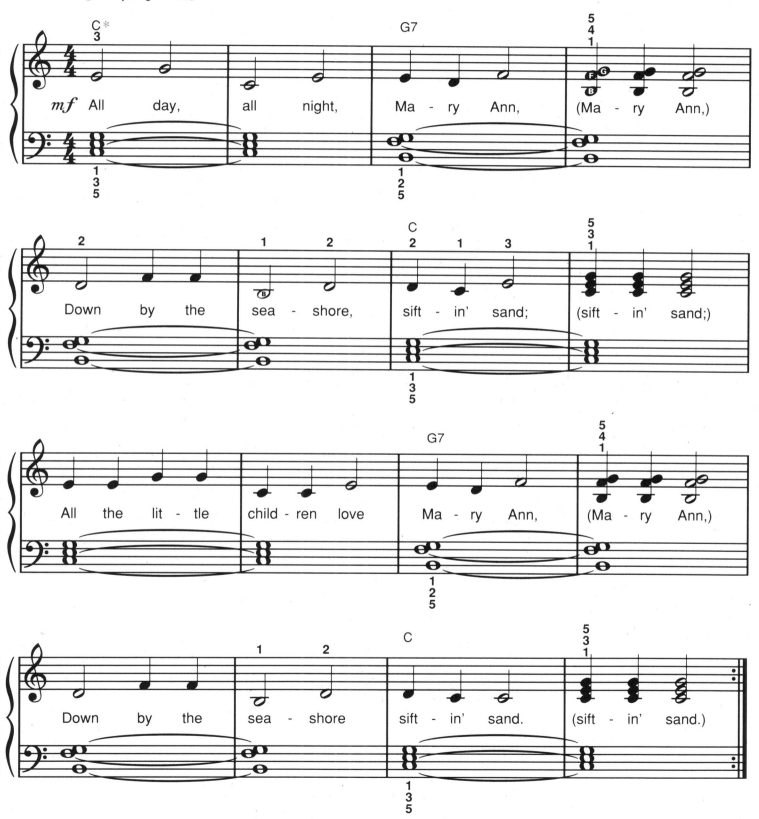

*In most popular sheet music, the chord symbols appear **ABOVE** the RH melody.
The symbol appears ONLY WHEN THE CHORD CHANGES.

New Time Signature

Dotted Half Note

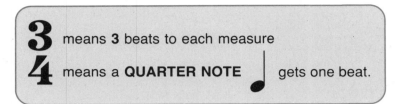

3 means **3** beats to each measure

4 means a **QUARTER NOTE** ♩ gets one beat.

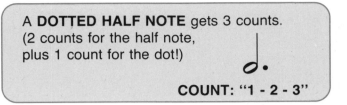

A **DOTTED HALF NOTE** gets 3 counts.
(2 counts for the half note,
plus 1 count for the dot!)

COUNT: "1 - 2 - 3"

Clap the following rhythm.

Clap **ONCE** for each note, counting aloud.

COUNT: 1   2   3   1   2   3   1   2   3   1   2   3

ROCKETS 🎵 Track 29

Begin at ♩ = 80 or slower.

Recording tempo ♩ = 120

On the recording, the piano part is played as described at the bottom of this page.

IMPORTANT! Play *ROCKETS* again, playing the 2nd line one octave (8 notes) higher.
The rests at the end of the 1st line give you time to move your hands to the new position!

WHAT CAN I SHARE? Track 30

Introducing Ⓐ for Left Hand

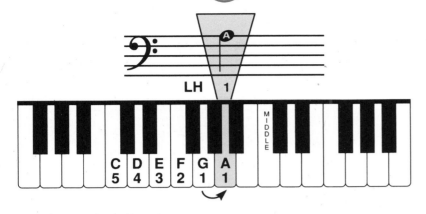

TO FIND A:

Place the LH in **C POSITION**.
Reach finger 1 one white key to the right!

Play slowly. Say the note names as you play.

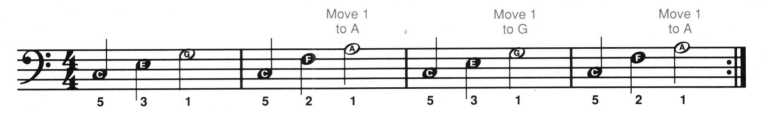

Introducing the F Major Chord

The C MAJOR chord is frequently followed by the F MAJOR chord, and vice-versa.

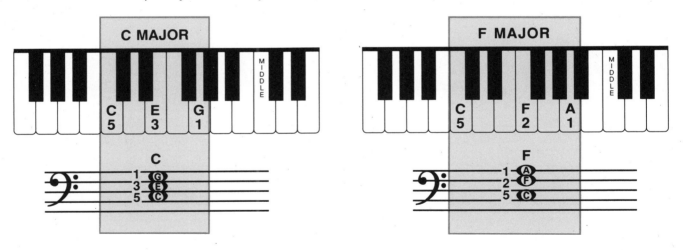

Practice changing from the C chord to the F chord and back again.

1. The 5th finger plays C in both chords.
2. The 2nd finger plays F in the F chord.
3. Only the 1st finger moves out of C POSITION (up to A) for the F chord.

IMPORTANT! To improve your skill at playing the F major chord, practice FINGER AEROBICS Nos. 12 & 13 on page 90.

Warm-Up using C, G⁷ & F Chords

Practice SLOWLY at first, then gradually increase speed.

> **INCOMPLETE MEASURE:**
>
> Some pieces begin with an INCOMPLETE MEASURE. The 1st measure of this piece has only 3 counts. The missing count is found in the last measure! When you repeat the whole song, you will have one whole measure of 4 counts when you play the last measure plus the first measure.

WHEN THE SAINTS GO MARCHING IN Track 31

When playing with the recording, begin after you hear one full measure plus one count (that is, after you hear 5 beats).

Recording tempo ♩ = 144

The Damper Pedal

The RIGHT PEDAL is called the **DAMPER PEDAL**.

When you hold the damper pedal down, any tone you sound will continue after you release the key.

Use the RIGHT FOOT on the damper pedal.
Always keep your heel on the floor. Use your ankle like a hinge.

This sign means: PEDAL DOWN   PEDAL UP
                                          HOLD PEDAL

HARP SONG   Track 32

Chords played one note at a time are called **BROKEN CHORDS**.
Many pieces are made entirely of broken chords, as this one is.

Begin as slowly as you wish. Recording tempo ♩ = 104.

Warm-Up using C, G⁷ & F Chords

This warm-up introduces a new way of playing **BROKEN CHORDS**.
Practice slowly at first. Increase speed to ♩ = 96.

BEAUTIFUL BROWN EYES

Track 33

Begin as slowly as you wish, but use your metronome.
Recording tempo ♩ = 96

Eighth Notes

Two eighth notes are played in the time of **one quarter note**.

When a piece contains eighth notes,

count: "**1 - &**" for each quarter note;
count: "**1 - &**" for each pair of eighth notes.

Eighth notes are usually played in **pairs.**

COUNT: "1 - &"

Clap these notes, counting aloud.

COUNT: 1 – &   2 – &   3 – &   4 – &   1 – &   2 – &   3 – &   4 – &

SKIP TO MY LOU   Track 34

Play this several times with RH alone, with your metronome. Begin at about ♩ = 80, or slower.

Recording tempo ♩ = 120

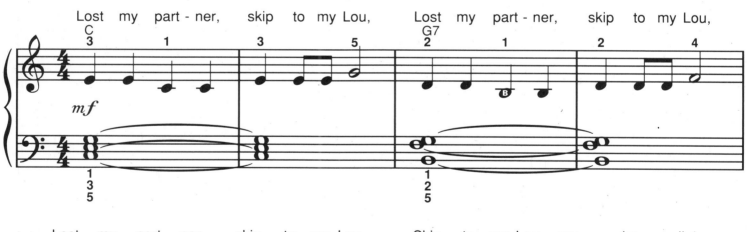

Broken Chord Warm-Up

Play this many times with metronome at ♩ = 80.

SKIP TO MY LOU   Track 35

Play LH alone at first, at ♩ = 80, then add the RH.
Increase tempo to ♩ = 120, then play with the recording.

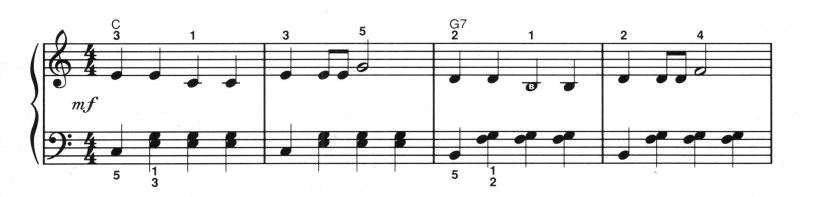

THE GIFT TO BE SIMPLE

Track 36

This sign is called a **FERMATA.**

Hold the note under the FERMATA longer than its value.

This beautiful old Shaker melody was used by the famous American composer, Aaron Copland, in his well known symphonic composition, *Appalachian Spring.*

When playing with the recording, begin after you hear one full measure plus three counts (after you hear 7 beats).

Recording tempo ♩ = 76

Introducing Dotted Quarter Notes

A DOT INCREASES THE LENGTH OF A NOTE BY ONE HALF ITS VALUE.

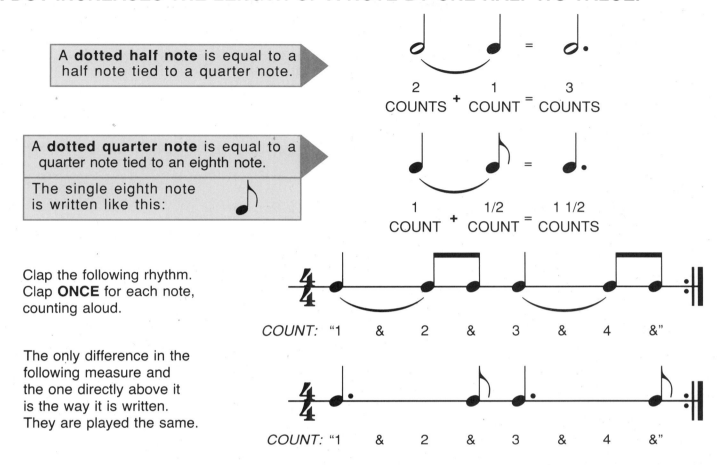

A **dotted half note** is equal to a half note tied to a quarter note.

A **dotted quarter note** is equal to a quarter note tied to an eighth note.

The single eighth note is written like this:

Clap the following rhythm. Clap **ONCE** for each note, counting aloud.

The only difference in the following measure and the one directly above it is the way it is written. They are played the same.

In $\frac{4}{4}$ or $\frac{3}{4}$ time, the DOTTED QUARTER NOTE is almost ALWAYS followed by an EIGHTH NOTE!

The following excerpts from well-known songs will show you the sound of the dotted quarter and eighth note rhythm.

On the recording, you will hear a 2 measure count-off before each example, the first in $\frac{3}{4}$ time, and the 2nd in $\frac{4}{4}$ time.

Recording tempo ♩ = 68

SILENT NIGHT Track 37

Si - lent night, Ho - ly night,

Recording tempo ♩ = 120

HERE COMES THE BRIDE Track 38

Here comes the bride! All dressed in white!

IMPORTANT! To improve your skill at playing dotted quarter and eighth notes, practice FINGER AEROBICS Nos. 14 & 15 on page 91.

ALOUETTE

 Track 39

Recording tempo ♩ = 104

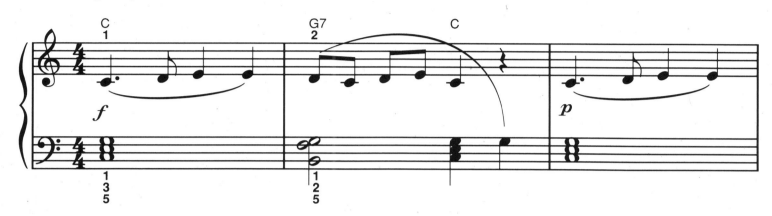

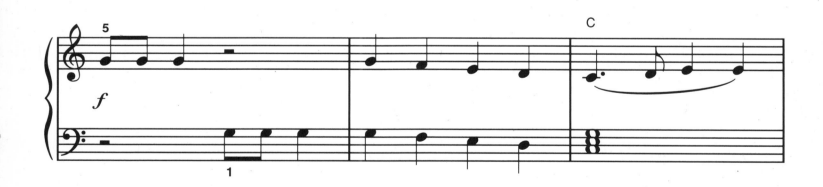

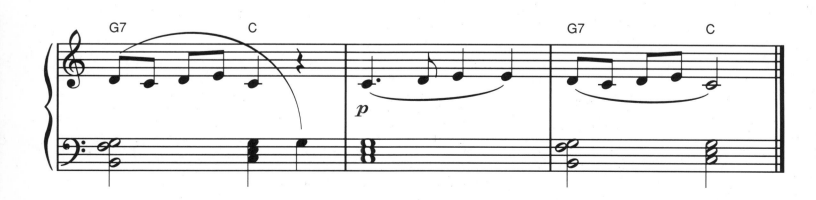

Measuring 6ths

When you skip 4 white keys,
the interval is a **6th**.

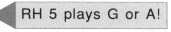
6th

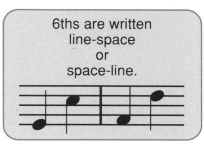
6ths are written
line-space
or
space-line.

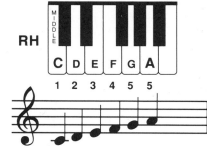

This is C POSITION plus 1 note (A) played with 5.

RH 5 plays G or A!

Say the names of these intervals as you play!

MELODIC INTERVALS:

HARMONIC INTERVALS:

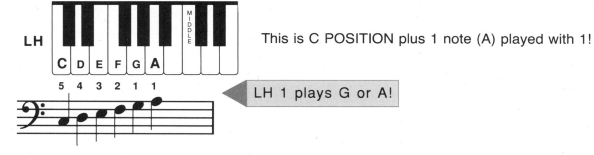

This is C POSITION plus 1 note (A) played with 1!

LH 1 plays G or A!

Say the names of these intervals as you play!

MELODIC INTERVALS:

HARMONIC INTERVALS:

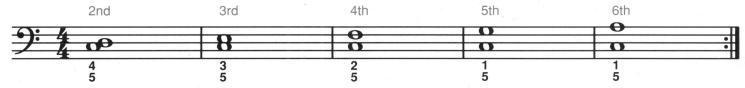

IMPORTANT! To improve your skill at playing 6ths, practice FINGER AEROBIC No. 16 on page 92. This is one of the finest exercises ever devised. It will also improve your ability to play equally well with all 5 fingers of the RH & LH.

48

In *LAVENDER'S BLUE,* 5ths and 6ths are played with 1 & 5.
Practice this WARM-UP, before playing *LAVENDER'S BLUE.*

LAVENDER'S BLUE Track 40

Recording tempo ♩ = 96

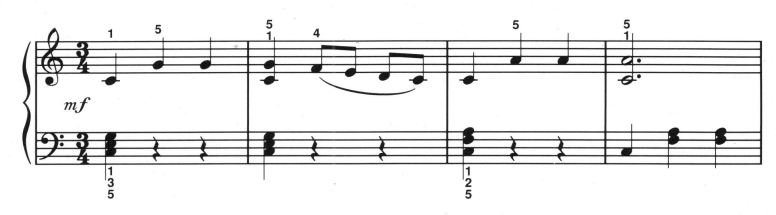

New Time Signature

2/4 means **2** beats to each measure.
2/4 means a **QUARTER NOTE** gets one beat.

This piece uses 2/4 and 4/4 time, changing time signatures in each measure.

Clap the following rhythm.
Clap ONCE for each note, counting aloud.

COUNT: " 1   2   1   2 & 3   4 "

KUM-BA-YAH!* 🔘 Track 41

When playing with the recording, begin after you hear 4 beats.
Recording tempo ♩ = 96

*Kum-ba-yah means "Come by here."

When you play in positions that include 6 or more notes, any finger may be required to play 2 notes.

LONDON BRIDGE Track 42

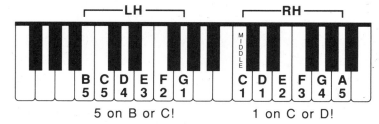

5 on B or C!   1 on C or D!

Recording tempo ♩ = 120

2nd time play RH 8va

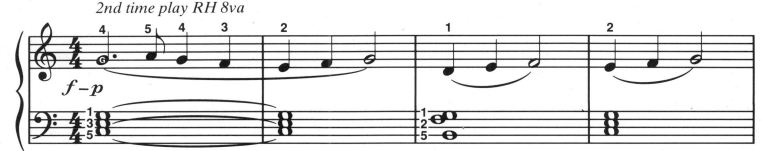

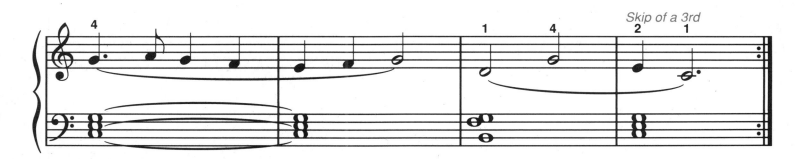

MICHAEL, ROW THE BOAT ASHORE Track 43

RH 1 plays C, 2 plays E.

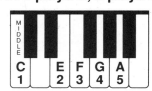

On the recording, you will hear a 2 measure rhythm intro.
When playing with the recording, begin after you hear one full measure plus two counts (after 6 beats).

Recording tempo ♩ = 104

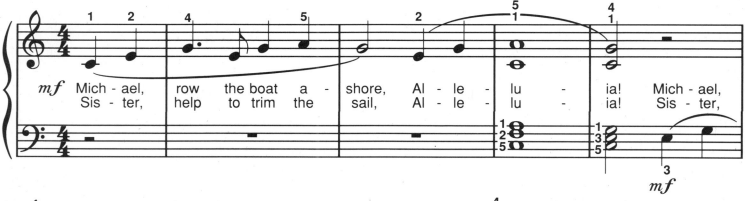

mf Mich - ael, row the boat a - shore, Al - le - lu - ia! Mich - ael,
Sis - ter, help to trim the sail, Al - le - lu - ia! Sis - ter,

row the boat a - shore, Al - le - lu - ia!
help to trim the sail, Al - le - lu - ia!

Syncopated Notes

Notes played between the main beats of the measure
and held across the beat are called **SYNCOPATED NOTES**.

Clap and count this rhythm several times.

SYNCOPATED NOTE

COUNT: 1 & 2 & 3 & 4 &

ROCK-A MY SOUL Track 44

Recording tempo ♩ = 120

* ♮ This is a natural sign. It cancels a sharp or flat. Play D. A natural note is always a white key

Moving Up & Down the Keyboard in 6ths

To play popular and classical music, you must be able to move freely over the keyboard. These exercises will prepare you to do this. Each hand plays 6ths, moving up and down the keyboard to neighboring keys. READ ONLY THE LOWEST NOTE OF EACH INTERVAL, adding a 6th above!

RH 6ths, MOVING FROM A/C UP TO E/G AND BACK.

Begin with RH 1 on MIDDLE C.

LH 6ths, MOVING FROM C/E DOWN TO F/A AND BACK.

Begin with LH 1 on MIDDLE C.

LONE STAR WALTZ Track 45

This piece combines the positions used in *LONDON BRIDGE* with MOVING UP & DOWN THE KEYBOARD IN 6ths.

Recording tempo ♩ = 96

2nd time both hands 8ᵛᵃ

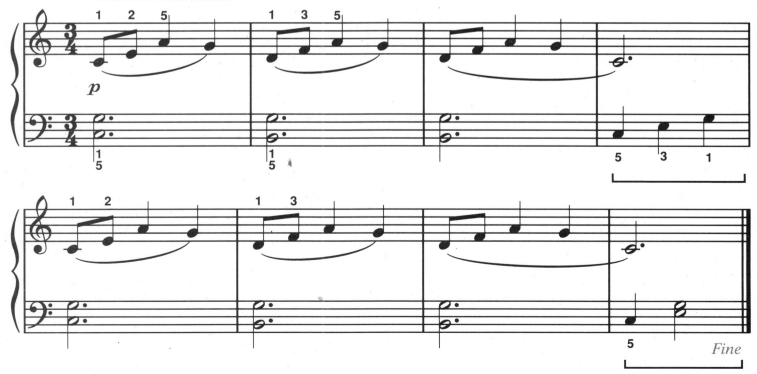

Fine

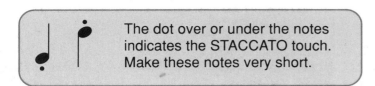

The dot over or under the notes indicates the STACCATO touch. Make these notes very short.

D.C. al Fine

D.C. al Fine (Da Capo al Fine) means repeat from the beginning and play to the end (*Fine*).

Measuring 7ths & Octaves

When you skip 5 white keys,
the interval is a **7th.**

When you skip 6 white keys,
the interval is an **OCTAVE.**

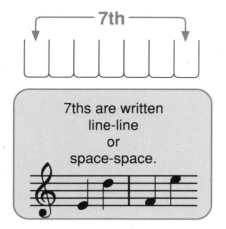

7ths are written
line-line
or
space-space.

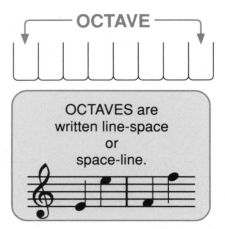

OCTAVES are
written line-space
or
space-line.

Say the names of these intervals as you play!

RH MELODIC INTERVALS:

RH HARMONIC INTERVALS:

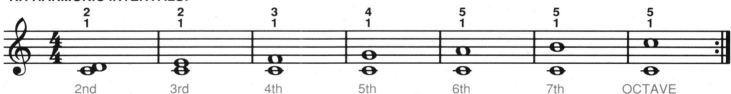

LH MELODIC INTERVALS:

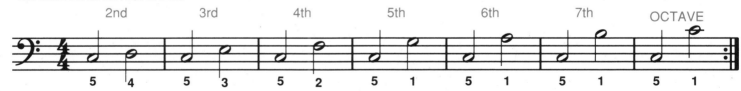

LH HARMONIC INTERVALS:

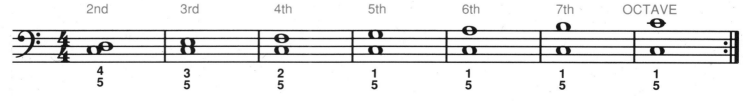

IMPORTANT! To improve your skill at playing melodic & harmonic intervals, 2nds through octaves, practice
FINGER AEROBICS Nos. 17, 18 & 19 on page 93.

Café Vienna

Track 46

Play hands separately at first, then together.
Be especially careful of the RH fingering! Notice that the 1st two notes,
a melodic 3rd, are played with 2 & 1!

Recording tempo ♩ = 104

Brahms' Lullaby Track 47

When playing with the recording, begin after you hear one full measure plus two counts (after you hear 5 beats). On the recording, the repeat is not observed. Play the 2nd ending.

Recording tempo ♩ = 66

Johannes Brahms

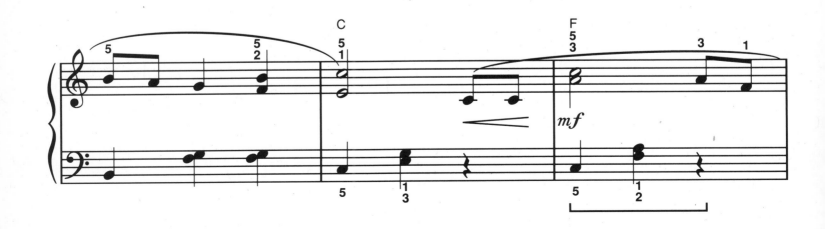

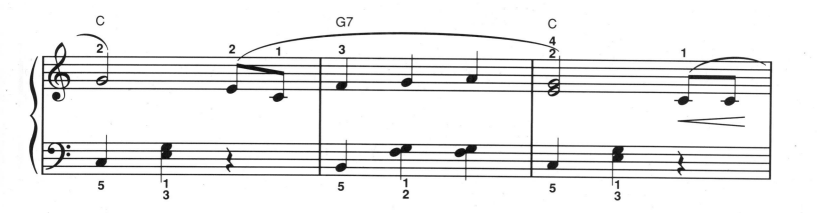

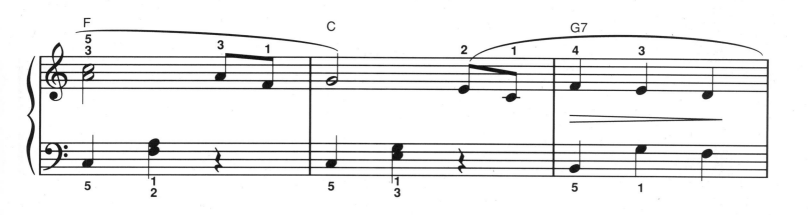

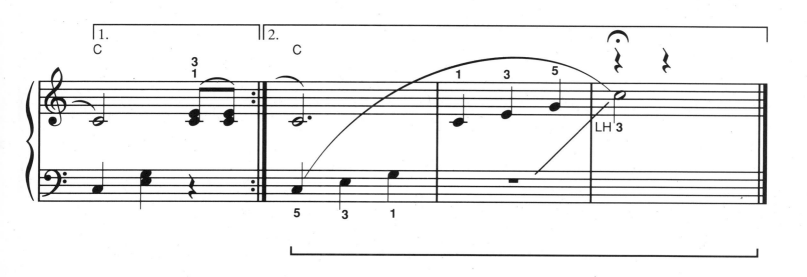

The Flat Sign

The **FLAT SIGN** before a note means play the next key to the LEFT, whether black or white.

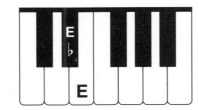

When a FLAT (♭) appears before a note, it applies to that note for the rest of the measure.

ROCK IT AWAY! Track 48

Recording tempo ♩ = 104

*1
C   F   3   2
f If you're feel-in' blue, if you're   feel-in' kind-a wear-y,
1
3
5   1
                                     2
                                     5

C   F   3 1 3   2
1
If you're feel-in' blue, bet-ter   hear what I say!
1
3
5   1   1
                                     2   2
                                     5   5

C   F   3
1
Play this rock-in' tune, it will   sure-ly make you cheer-y;
1
3
5   1
                                     2
                                     5

C   F   G7   C
1   3 1   2   1
When you feel in trou-ble, just   rock it   a - way!
1
3   1   1
5   2   2
                                     5   5

*The eighth notes may be played a bit unevenly: long short long short, etc.

Measuring Half Steps & Whole Steps

Half Steps

A **HALF STEP** is the distance from any key to the very next key above or below (black or white).

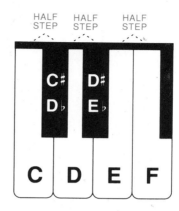

HALF STEPS · NO KEY BETWEEN

Whole Steps

A **WHOLE STEP** is equal to 2 half steps. Skip one key (black or white).

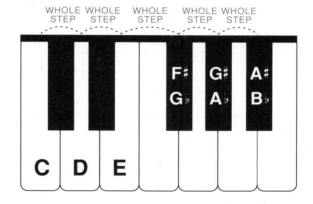

WHOLE STEPS · ONE KEY BETWEEN

Tetrachords

A **TETRACHORD** is a series of **FOUR NOTES** having a pattern of:

WHOLE STEP, WHOLE STEP, HALF STEP.

The notes of a tetrachord must be in alphabetical order ⟶

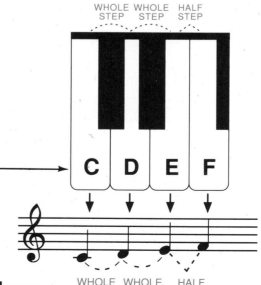

and must also have this pattern! ⟶ WHOLE STEP WHOLE STEP HALF STEP

The Major Scale

The MAJOR SCALE is made of **TWO TETRACHORDS** *joined* by a **WHOLE STEP.**

The C MAJOR SCALE is constructed as follows:

> There is NO ♯ OR ♭
> in the **C MAJOR SCALE.**

Each scale begins and ends on a note of the same name as the scale, called the **KEY NOTE.**

Preparation for Scale Playing

IMPORTANT!   Since there are EIGHT notes in the C MAJOR SCALE and we have only **FIVE** fingers, an important trick must be mastered: **passing the thumb under the 3rd finger!** This exercise will make this trick easy.

Play HANDS SEPARATELY. Begin VERY SLOWLY. Keep the wrist loose and quiet!

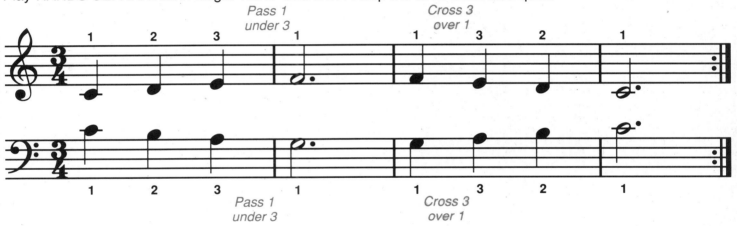

The C Major Scale

Begin SLOWLY. **Lean** the hand slightly in the direction you are moving. The hand should move smoothly along with no twisting motion of the wrist!

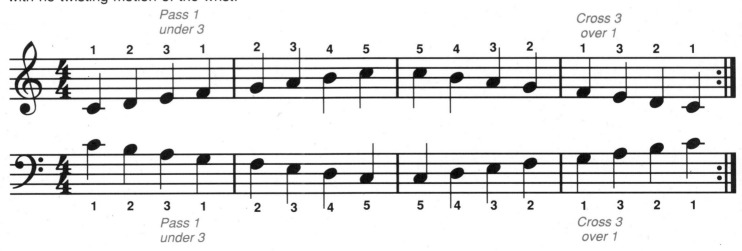

IMPORTANT! To improve your skill at playing scales, practice FINGER AEROBICS Nos. 20 & 21 on page 94.

JOY TO THE WORLD

 Track 49

Scales occur often in melodies.
This favorite melody is made up almost entirely of major scales.

When playing with the recording, hold the fermata for 7 counts.

Recording tempo ♩ = 140

G. F. Handel

More About Chords

A TRIAD IS A 3-NOTE CHORD.

THE THREE NOTES OF A TRIAD ARE:

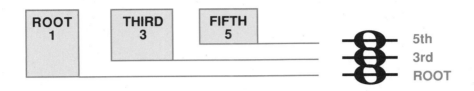

The ROOT is the note from which the triad gets its name. The ROOT of a C triad is C.

TRIADS IN **ROOT POSITION** (WITH ROOT AT THE BOTTOM)
ALWAYS LOOK LIKE THIS:

OR THIS:

TRIADS MAY BE BUILT ON ANY NOTE OF ANY SCALE.

TRIADS BUILT ON THE C MAJOR SCALE

Play with RH

Play with LH

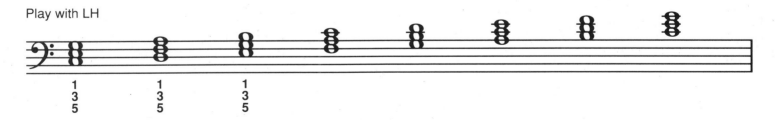

LISTEN CAREFULLY TO THE SOUND OF THESE ROOT POSITION TRIADS!

When you name the notes of any **TRIAD IN ROOT POSITION,** you will always skip **ONE** letter of the musical alphabet between each note. The triads you played above are:

C E G   D F A   E G B   F A C   G B D   A C E   B D F

This is the complete **"TRIAD VOCABULARY!"** It should be memorized!

COCKLES AND MUSSELS 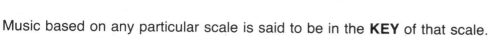 Track 50

Music based on any particular scale is said to be in the **KEY** of that scale.

If there are sharps or flats in the scale, they are shown at the beginning of the music.
This is called the **KEY SIGNATURE.**

Play LH alone at a very slow tempo before playing hands together.
When playing with the recording, begin after you hear one full measure plus 2 counts (after you hear 5 beats.)

Recording tempo ♩ = 120

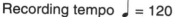

The Primary Chords in C Major

The 3 most important chords in any key are those built on the 1st, 4th, & 5th notes of the scale. These are called the **PRIMARY CHORDS** of the key.

The chords are identified by the Roman numerals **I, IV, & V** (1, 4, & 5).
The **V** chord usually adds the note a 7th above the root to make a V^7 (5-7) chord.

In the key of C MAJOR, the **I CHORD** is the C MAJOR TRIAD.
The **IV CHORD** is the F MAJOR TRIAD.
The **V^7 CHORD** is the G^7 CHORD (G major triad with an added 7th).

THE PRIMARY CHORDS IN C MAJOR:

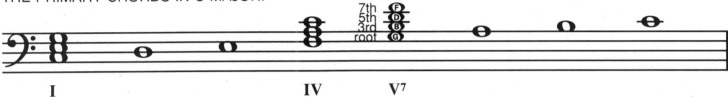

Chord Progressions

When we change from one chord to another, we call this a "CHORD PROGRESSION."

When all chords are in root position, the hand must leap from one chord to the next. To make the chord progressions easier to play and sound better, the **IV** and **V^7** chords may be played in other positions by moving one or more of the higher chord tones down an octave.

The **I** chord is played in ROOT POSITION:

The top note of the **IV** chord is moved down an octave:

In the **V^7** chord, the 5th (D) is usually omitted. All notes except the root are moved down an octave.

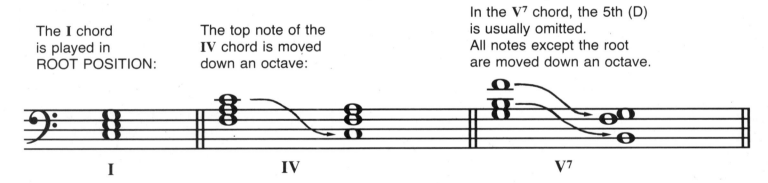

The 3 PRIMARY CHORDS are then comfortably played as follows:

It is important that you now think of the C, F & G^7 chords in the key of C MAJOR as the I, IV & V^7 chords!

Play the following line several times, saying the numerals of each chord as you play.

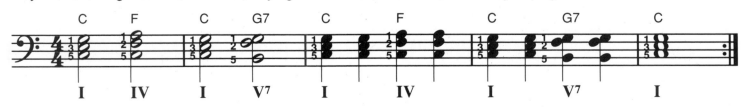

WALKIN' DOWN THE BASSES Track 51

In this piece you will play all the notes of the bass staff, while reviewing the I, IV & V7 chords in the treble staff.

CHANGING LH FINGERS ON REPEATED NOTES:

Notice a special fingering trick used in going from measure 1 to measure 2. The last note of the 1st measure is played with LH 4. The first note of the 2nd measure is the same note, but it is played with LH 1, allowing the hand to continue down the staff. The same thing happens between measures 3 & 4.

Play the LH alone several times, at ♩ = 72, or slower.

Recording tempo ♩ = 120

*Speak these words loudly when performing.

The rhythm between the two hands may be played "long-short."

IMPORTANT! To improve your skill at changing fingers on repeated notes practice FINGER AEROBIC No. 22 on page 95.

About the Blues

Music called BLUES has long been a part of the American musical heritage. We find it in the music of many popular song writers, in ballads, boogie, and rock.

FORMULA FOR THE BLUES:

There are 12 measures in one "chorus" of the blues:

4 measures of the **I** chord; 2 measures of the **IV** chord; 2 measures of the **I** chord;
1 measure of the **V⁷** chord; 1 measure of the **IV** chord; 2 measures of the **I** chord.

This formula may be varied slightly. In I'M A WINNER, for example, measures 7 & 8 and measures 11 & 12 alternate back and forth between the I and IV chords, just to make the music more interesting. The basic harmony of these measures is still the I chord, which begins and ends each pair of measures.

In the measures mentioned above, the LH chords are broken in a new way.
Practice the following LH exercise before playing the piece.

KEY OF C MAJOR
Key Signature: no ♯, no ♭.

I'M A WINNER! Track 52

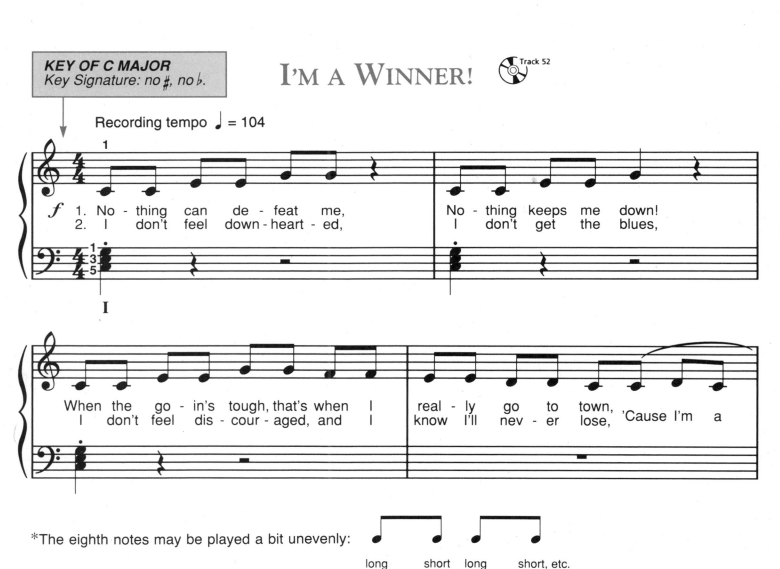

Recording tempo ♩ = 104

1. No - thing can de - feat me, No - thing keeps me down!
2. I don't feel down - heart - ed, I don't get the blues,

When the go - in's tough, that's when I real - ly go to town,
I don't feel dis - cour - aged, and I know I'll nev - er lose, 'Cause I'm a

*The eighth notes may be played a bit unevenly:

long short long short, etc.

win - ner! A win - ner! And let me tell you why I

IV

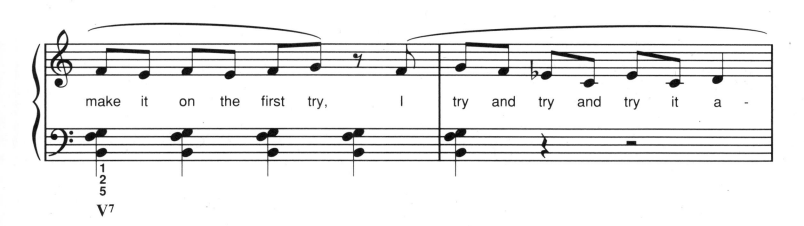

win: If I don't

I IV I IV I IV I

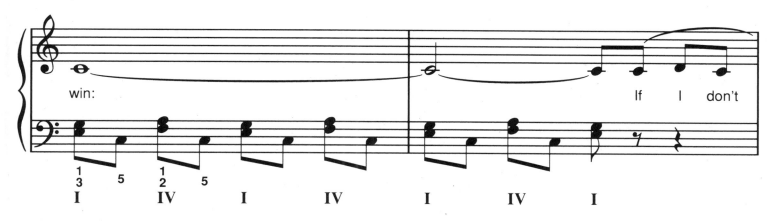

make it on the first try, I try and try and try it a -

V7

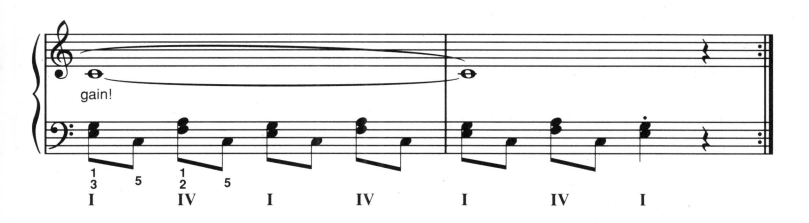

gain!

I IV I IV I IV I

Grace Notes

In music of all kinds, and especially in BLUES, small notes called "GRACE NOTES" (♪) are often used to "embellish" or decorate musical ideas to make them more effective.

Grace notes have no definite time value. They are played VERY QUICKLY, almost at the same time as the following large note. Try the following with RH alone.

Musical ideas without grace notes: Same ideas with grace notes added:

BLUES CITY Track 53

Recording tempo ♩ = 104

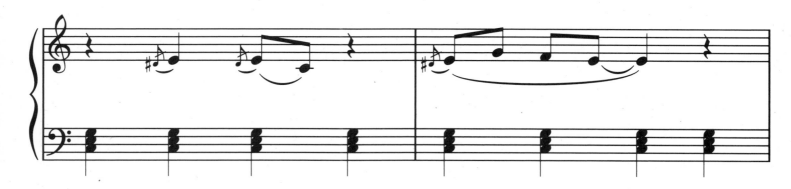

*The eighth notes may be played a bit unevenly:

long   short   long   short, etc.

RH: An Extended Position

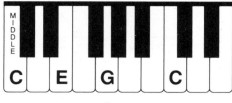

ON TOP OF OLD SMOKY begins and ends with the RH in an EXTENDED POSITION.

Play several times:

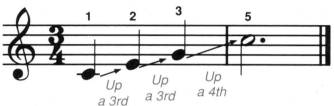

LH Review: BLOCK CHORDS & BROKEN CHORDS IN C

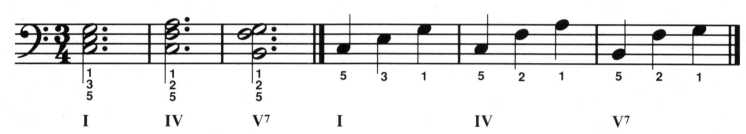

ON TOP OF OLD SMOKY Track 54

When playing with the recording, begin after you hear one full measure plus two counts (after you hear 5 beats).

Recording tempo ♩ = 104

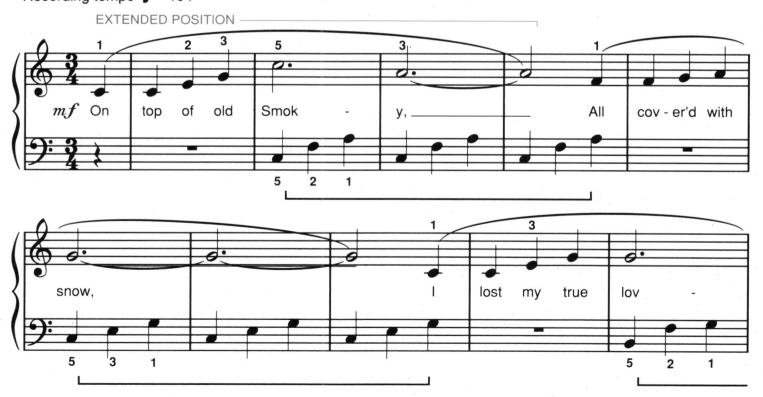

IMPORTANT! To improve your skill at playing in extended positions practice FINGER AEROBIC No. 24 on page 95.

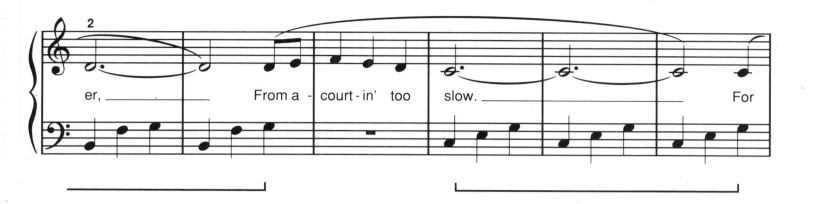

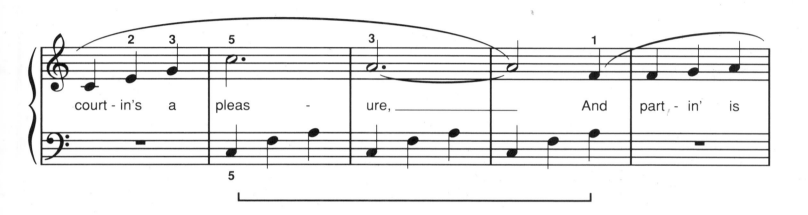

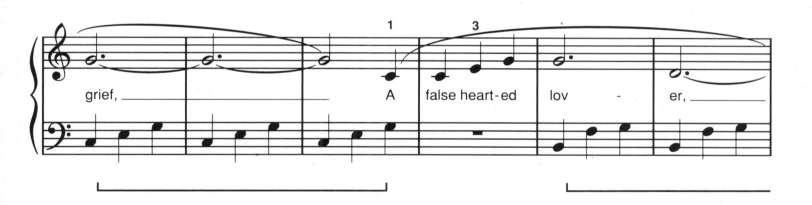

The G Major Scale

Remember that the MAJOR SCALE is made up of two tetrachords *joined* by a whole step.

The 2nd TETRACHORD of the G MAJOR SCALE begins on D.

> There is ONE # (F#)
> in the G MAJOR SCALE.

The Key of G Major

A piece based on the G Major scale is in the **KEY OF G MAJOR.**
Since F is sharp in the G scale, every F will be sharp in the key of G Major.

Instead of placing a sharp before every F in the entire piece,
the sharp is indicated at the beginning in the KEY SIGNATURE.

Practice the G MAJOR SCALE with HANDS SEPARATE.
Begin SLOWLY. Keep the wrist loose and quiet.

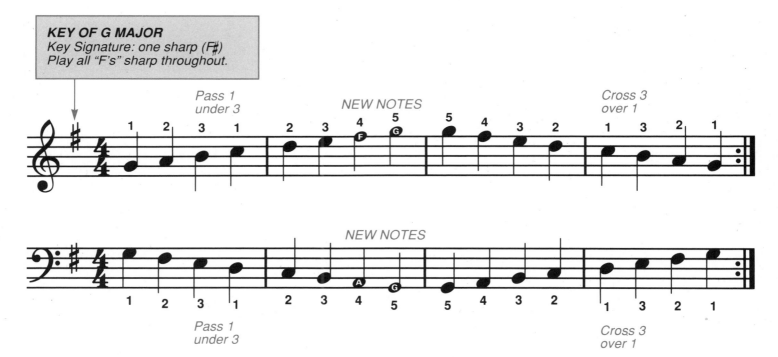

IMPORTANT! After you have learned the G MAJOR SCALE with hands separate, you may play the hands together. When the scale is played as written on the staffs above, the LH descends as the RH ascends, and vice versa. This is called CONTRARY MOTION—both hands play the SAME NUMBERED fingers at the same time!

You may also play, the C MAJOR SCALE at the bottom of page 60 with the hands together, in CONTRARY MOTION!

How to Make Any Major Triad

The **1st, 3rd, & 5th** notes of any **MAJOR SCALE** make a **MAJOR TRIAD**. It would not be difficult to find any major triad you choose by constructing the major scale of the chosen note, and then playing the 1st, 3rd, & 5th notes of the scale.

Here is a **QUICKER** and **EASIER** way to find **ANY** MAJOR TRIAD!

Choose any note as the **ROOT**.
Count up **2 whole steps** for the **3rd**.
Count up **1½ steps** more for the **5th**.

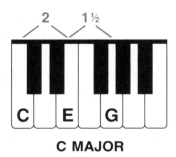

C MAJOR

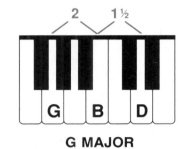

G MAJOR

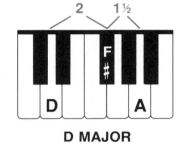

D MAJOR

Play each of the above 3 triads in several places on the keyboard, using RH 1 3 5. Carefully observe that there are 2 whole steps between the ROOT and the 3rd, and 1½ steps between the 3rd and the 5th. Repeat, using LH 5 3 1.

How to Play I–V⁷ Progressions Beginning on Any Major Triad

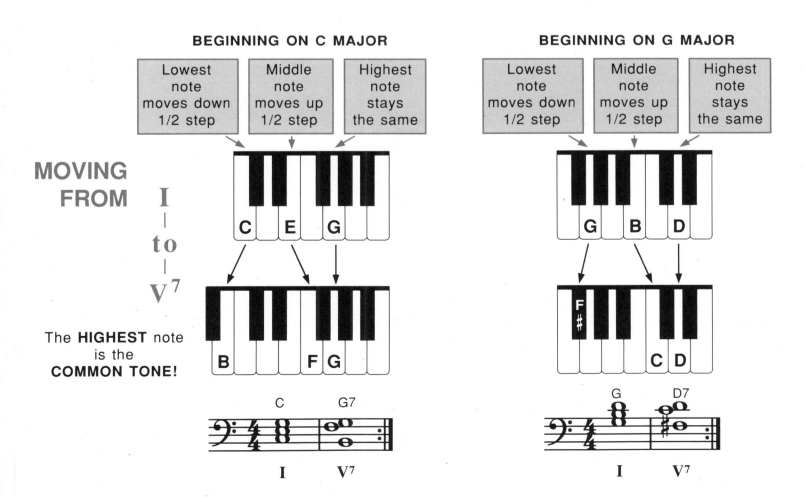

THE CAN-CAN  Track 55

Practice first with LH alone. Remember, all F's are SHARP.

CHANGING RH FINGERS ON REPEATED NOTES:

In this piece the RH does the special fingering trick you learned with the LH on page 65. See the fingering indications in measures 3, 4, 5 & 6.

Practice the RH alone before playing hands together. Be sure to make all F's SHARP!

J. Offenbach

How to Play I–IV Progressions Beginning on Any Major Triad

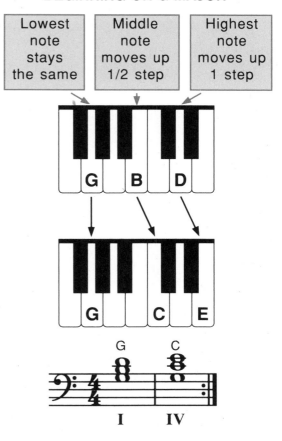

BEGINNING ON C MAJOR

Lowest note stays the same	Middle note moves up 1/2 step	Highest note moves up 1 step

MOVING FROM I — to — IV

C E G → C F A

The **LOWEST** note is the **COMMON TONE!**

C — I   F — IV

BEGINNING ON G MAJOR

Lowest note stays the same	Middle note moves up 1/2 step	Highest note moves up 1 step

G B D → G C E

G — I   C — IV

The Primary Chords in G Major

Reviewing the G MAJOR SCALE, LH ascending.

KEY OF G MAJOR
Key Signature: one sharp (F♯)

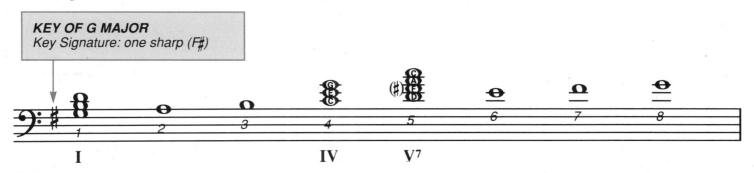

I   IV   V⁷

The following chord positions (which you have already learned) are used for smooth progressions:

Primary Chords in G

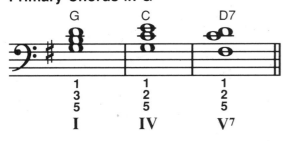

G	C	D7
1 3 5	1 2 5	1 2 5
I	IV	V⁷

G Major Chord Progression with I, IV, & V⁷ Chords.
Play several times, saying the numerals aloud:

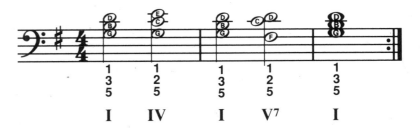

I   IV   I   V⁷   I

THE MARINES' HYMN Track 56

When playing with the recording, begin after you hear one full measure plus three counts (after you hear 7 beats.)

Recording tempo ♩ = 96

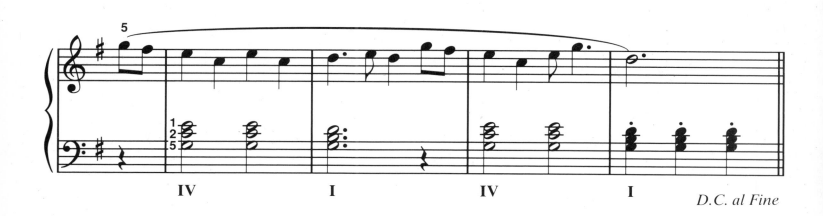

Fine

D.C. al Fine

Broken Chords in G Major

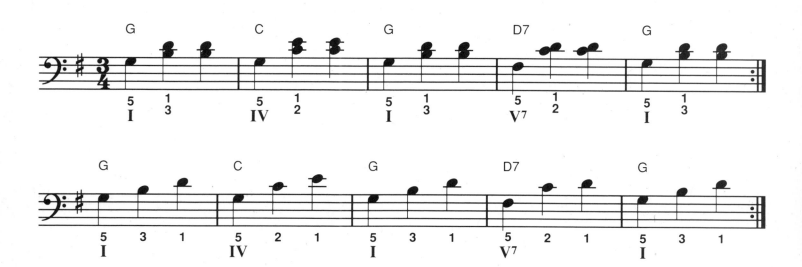

Plaisir d'Amour
(The Joy of Love)

 Track 57

This piece was made into a popular song by Elvis Presley.

Make this piece easier by practicing the LH alone at first, at a slow tempo.

When playing with the recording, begin after you hear one full measure plus two counts (after you hear 5 beats).

Recording tempo ♩ = 104

Giovanni Martini

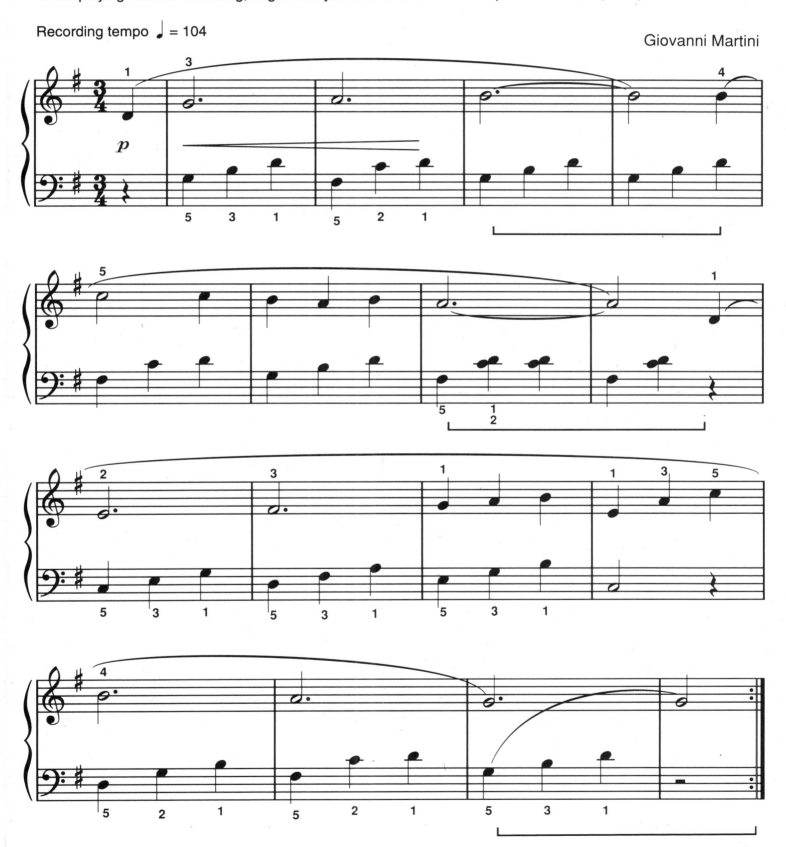

A New Style of Bass

Play this several times before beginning *O SOLE MIO:*

Begin at ♩ = 50. Gradually increase speed to ♩ = 96.

COUNT: 1 & 2 & 3 & 4 &   1 & 2 & 3 & 4 &   1 & 2 & 3 & 4 &   1 & 2 & 3 & 4 &

O SOLE MIO! Track 58

This great old favorite has provided tenors with sure-fire encore material, from Enrico Caruso to José Carreras, Placido Domingo and Luciano Pavarotti (recorded by them "In Concert"). "There's No Tomorrow," popular in the 50's and 60's, was sung to this melody.

When playing with the recording, begin after you hear one full measure plus one count. Hold the first three RH chords for 2 counts each (because of the fermatas). In the next to last full measure, hold the fermata for 3 1/2 counts.

Recording tempo ♩ = 96

E. di Capua

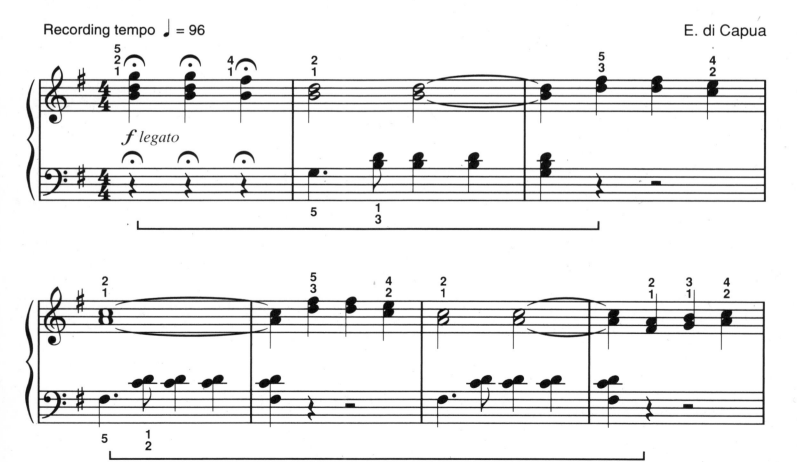

*Note the E♭ in the C chord. This changes the **IV** chord to a MINOR chord.

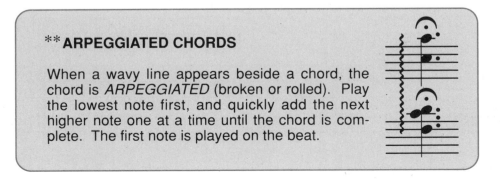

**ARPEGGIATED CHORDS

When a wavy line appears beside a chord, the chord is *ARPEGGIATED* (broken or rolled). Play the lowest note first, and quickly add the next higher note one at a time until the chord is complete. The first note is played on the beat.

LH Warm-Up

Practice many times, very slowly. These 4 measures contain everything new that you will find in the LH of *THE ENTERTAINER!*

THE ENTERTAINER

Scott Joplin

Not fast!*   Recording tempo ♩ = 96

*"Not fast" is the composer's own indication!

Eighth Note Triplets

When three notes are grouped together with a figure "3" above or below the notes, the group is called a **TRIPLET**.

The THREE NOTES of an
EIGHTH NOTE TRIPLET GROUP = ONE QUARTER NOTE.

When a piece contains triplets, count "TRIP-A-LET"

Amazing Grace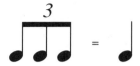

This piece will be easier if you practice the hands separately at first.
You may even wish to play each hand separately along with the recording.

When you play with the recording, begin after you hear one full measure plus two counts (after you hear 5 beats).

Recording tempo ♩ = 72

John Newton, J. Carrell, & D. Clayton

simile = "same." This means continue playing in the same manner. In this case, continue to play triplets each time three eighth notes are joined with one beam.

IMPORTANT! To improve your skill at playing eighth note triplets practice FINGER AEROBICS Nos. 25 & 26 on page 96.

The Problem of Developing Equal Skills with All Fingers

By this time you will realize that some fingers are more difficult to control than others.

The 5th finger is the smallest and weakest, and requires special exercise to develop strength equal to the others.

The 4th finger is the least independent finger, and the least agile. It is the only finger that is bound to its neighboring fingers by tendons that limit its movement.

The 3rd and 2nd fingers are the most agile fingers. They can move more easily through a larger arc. They are the strongest fingers.

The 1st finger (thumb) has its own problems. Its muscles are not designed to make it easy to strike a downward arc, but rather to pull the thumb inward, toward the palm. This makes it practical to turn the thumb under the fingers for playing scales, as you will see later, but in ordinary playing the thumb must strike on the side-tip, and is thus more awkward than the other fingers.

The following illustration shows the tendons of the left hand, as viewed from the back of the hand.

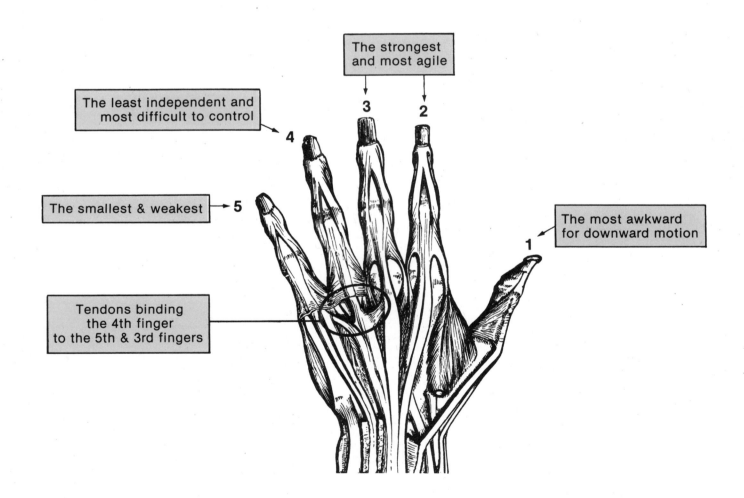

Illustration from "Gray's Anatomy"

More Finger "Aerobics"

No. 2
This exercise is a challenge for the weaker fingers (4–5).
These fingers will be strengthened with a little extra practice.

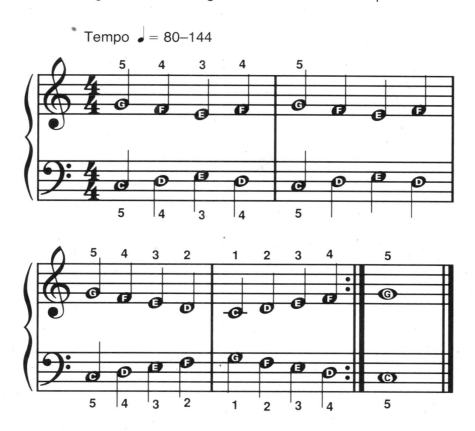

No. 3

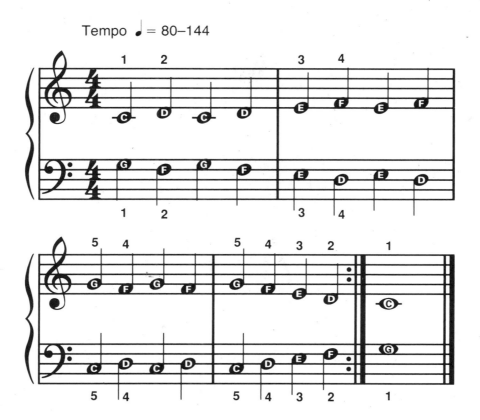

No. 4 Drops & Lifts on 2nds

DROP on the first key of each slurred pair.
Let the wrist lead the hand as you LIFT off of the end note of each pair.

Practice first at ♩ = 80. Gradually increase speed to ♩ = 120.

p-mf-f means play *soft* the first time, *moderately loud* the second time, and *loud* the third time.

Play each line 3 times.

No. 5 Drops & Lifts on 3rds

DROP into the first note, and LIFT off of the 2nd note of each slurred pair.

Begin at ♩ = 80. Gradually increase speed to ♩ = 120.

No. 6 Drops & Lifts

On Melodic 2nds, 3rds, 4ths, & 5ths

No. 7 Drops & Lifts

On Harmonic 2nds, 3rds, 4ths & 5ths

COUNT: "DROP - LIFT - 3 - 4," etc.

Drops & Lifts On C Major Chords

IMPORTANT! Shape your hands (in the air) to play the correct keys before you begin each exercise. The fingers and wrists should be relaxed, not stiff.

LH (MIRROR IMAGES) **RH**

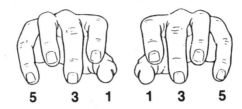

5   3   1   1   3   5

No. 8 Alternating Hands

Lift hands high (8 to 12 inches above the keyboard).
You may depress the right pedal, known as the *DAMPER PEDAL*, and hold it throughout the exercise, if you wish.
This will cause the chords to continue to sound after they are released.

COUNT: "DROP-TWO-LIFT-FOUR,   DROP-TWO-LIFT-FOUR," *etc.*

No. 9 Hands Together, Changing Octaves

To make sure the wrists are relaxed, move the hands loosely up and down,
as if waving "good-bye," before you play.
DROP into each chord with pre-shaped, but relaxed fingers.
Lift the hands high for each rest, and move to the new octave position.
You may hold the damper pedal down, if you wish.

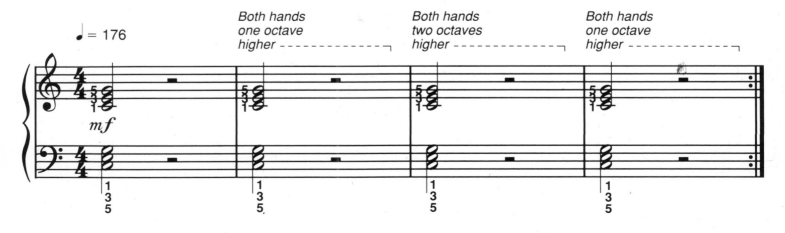

Both hands one octave higher - - - - - - - - - - - - ‾| Both hands two octaves higher - - - - - - - - - ‾| Both hands one octave higher - - - - - - - - - - - ‾|

Drops & Lifts on G⁷ Chords

IMPORTANT! Shape your hands (in the air) to play the correct keys before you begin each exercise. Always keep fingers and wrists relaxed.

LH (MIRROR IMAGES) **RH**

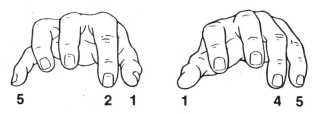

No. 10 Alternating Hands

Lift hands High
You may hold the damper pedal down, if you wish.

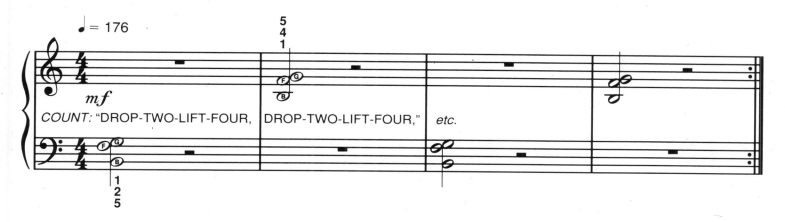

COUNT: "DROP-TWO-LIFT-FOUR, DROP-TWO-LIFT-FOUR," *etc.*

No. 11 Hands Together, Changing Octaves

Lift hands high.
You may hold the damper pedal down, if you wish.

Slow to Moderately slow

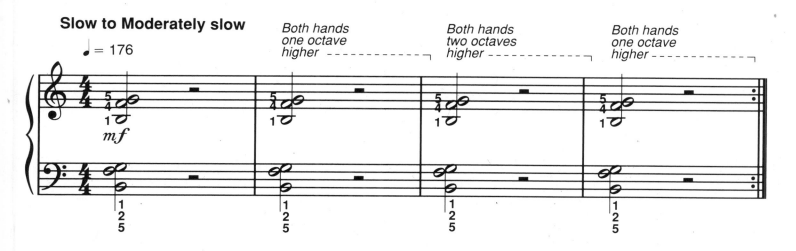

Drops & Lifts on F Major Chords

IMPORTANT! Shape your hands (in the air) to play the correct keys before you begin each exercise.
Always keep fingers and wrists relaxed.

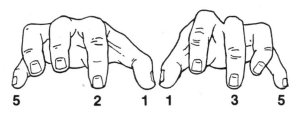

LH (MIRROR IMAGES) **RH**

No. 12 **Alternating Hands**

Lift hands high.
You may hold the damper pedal down, if you wish.

No. 13 **Hands Together, Changing Octaves**

Lift hands high.
You may hold the damper pedal down, if you wish.

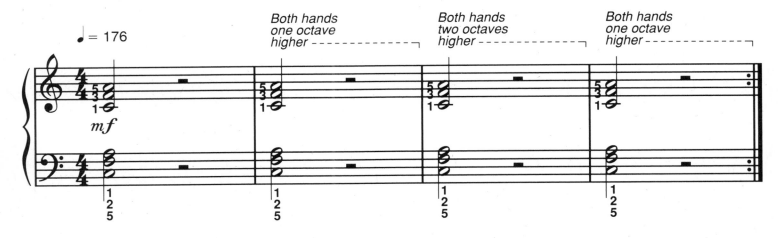

Dotted Aerobics

No. 14 **Dotted Rhythms**

♩ = 120

2nd TIME PLAY BOTH HANDS 1 OCTAVE LOWER

No. 15 **Chords with Dotted Rhythms**

Position the hands over each chord before playing. Repeat the chords by using flexible wrists. LIFT on the half-rests, moving over the next chord in advance.

The rhythm is the same as "Here Comes the Bride!" Play boldly, with confidence.

♩ = 120

2nd TIME PLAY BOTH HANDS 1 OCTAVE HIGHER

No. 16 Hanon's Amazing Aerobic Sixth

Charles-Louis Hanon, pronounced "ah-NON" (1819–1900), wrote, "The 4th and 5th fingers are almost useless because of the lack of special exercises to strengthen them." He then proceeded to devise some exercises that are so successful that they brought him worldwide fame. They are still used as warm-ups by the most skilled pianists of the present day.

This exercise will make you thoroughly familiar with the interval of a 6th, at the same time giving all fingers a great workout! Notice how cleverly Hanon uses the 6th to raise the hands to the next higher position, then to lower them back again.

LIFT FINGERS HIGH. Play each note clearly and distinctly. Practice slowly, then gradually increase speed.

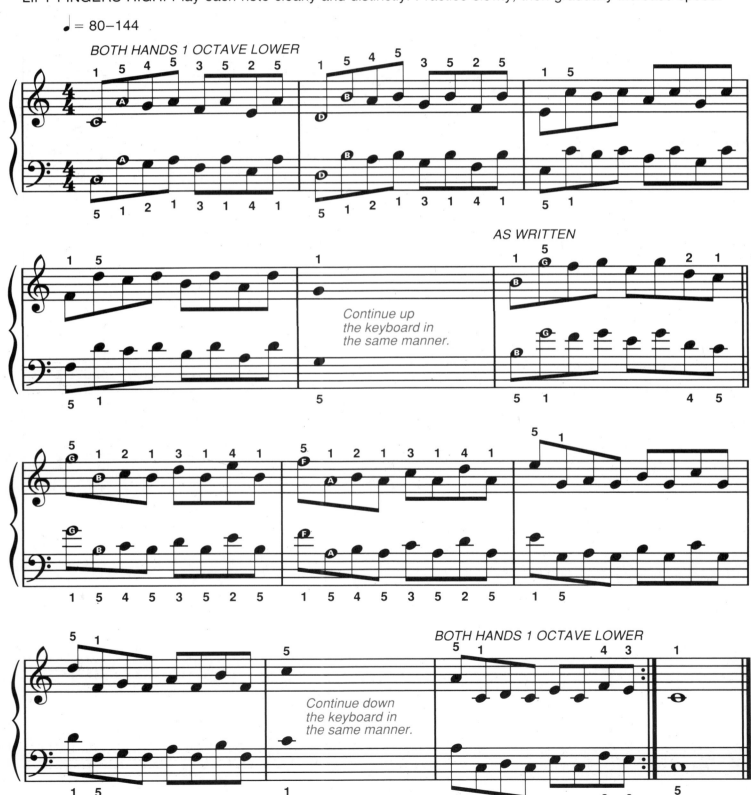

Stretching Exercises: 2nds to Octaves

Practice hands separately at first, then together.

No. 17 **Melodic Intervals**

No. 18 **Harmonic Intervals**

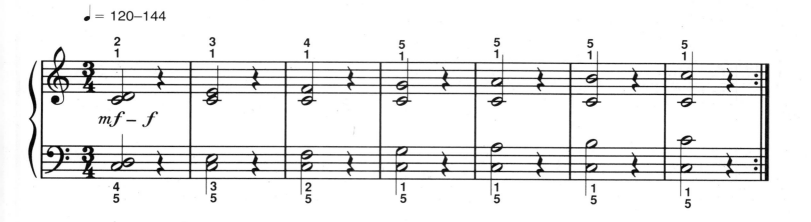

No. 19 **Staccato Notes**

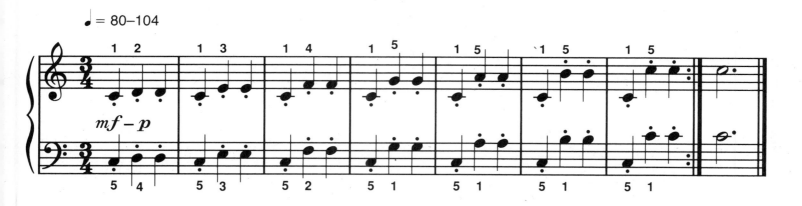

Scale Aerobics

These exercises will make scale playing easy.
Practice them daily, for several weeks.

No. 20 Thumb-Unders

Start the thumb-under motion just as you play the harmonic 2nd on the 2nd beat of each measure. The thumb should be over the key played on the 3rd beat well in advance. Keep the wrist loose and quiet. LIFT OFF on the 4th count.

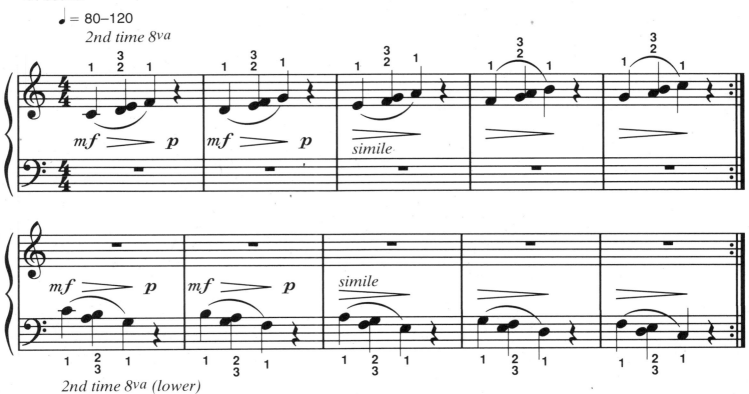

No. 21 Get Ready—Go!

Notice how easily you play the scale after playing the first two measures of each line!
Lean the hand slightly in the direction you are moving. Avoid any twisting motion of the wrists.

Changing Fingers on Repeated Notes

Fingers are sometimes changed on repeated notes for one of the following reasons:

1. To enable the hand to move gradually from one position to another.
2. To avoid tension in the wrist, which sometimes occurs when notes are rapidly repeated with the same finger.

No. 22   Begin at ♩ = 60 or slower. Gradually increase speed to ♩ = 120.

No. 23   Begin at ♩ = 80 or slower. Gradually increase speed to ♩ = 160.

Extended Positions

When the hand plays a four note chord made up of the ROOT, 3rd, 5th & OCTAVE, an EXTENDED POSITION must be used.

When the chord uses white keys only, the RH fingering is 1 2 3 5.
The LH fingering is 5 4 2 1.

No. 24   Begin at ♩ = 80 or slower. Gradually increase speed to ♩ = 144.

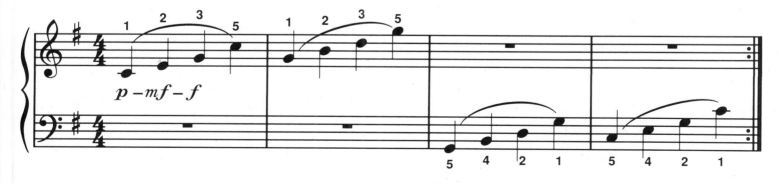

Eighth Note Triplets

Practicing scales in triplets will not only improve your understanding of triplet rhythm, but will also vastly improve your scale playing and your technic in general.

1. Play the hands separately at first, accenting the first note of each triplet.
   Begin at ♩ = 60 or slower. Gradually increase speed to ♩ = 120.

2. When you can play the hands separately very evenly throughout, begin to play hands together, very slowly at first. Observe the fact that 3rd fingers of both hands ALWAYS PLAY TOGETHER! These numbers are circled in the scales below, so you can clearly see how they coincide.

   Gradually increase speed. The faster you can play these scales, the better. But always be sure you can hear every note clearly, and that the triplets are smooth and evenly spaced. There should be no unevenness when the thumbs go under or the 3rd fingers go over.

No. 25   THE C MAJOR SCALE in triplet rhythm.

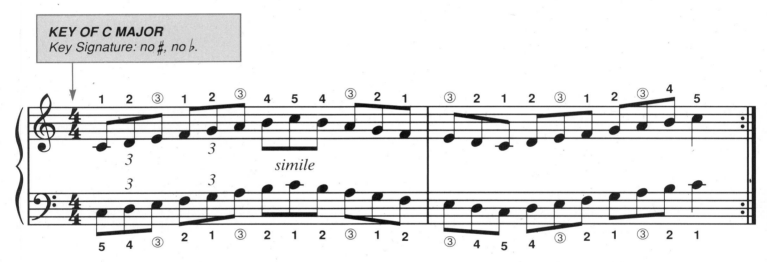

No. 26   THE G MAJOR SCALE in triplet rhythm.

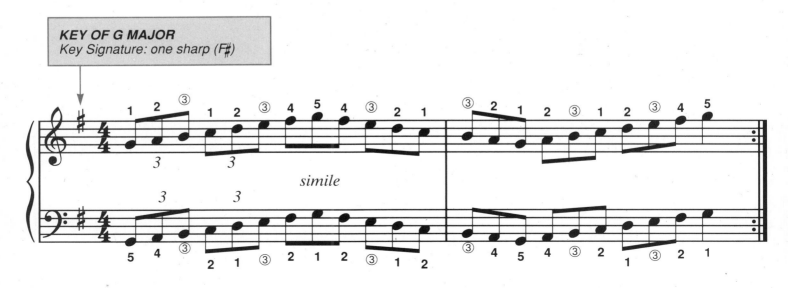